Profits for All:
Flexible Wages
in a Free Economy

Michael Szpindor Watson and Grattan Brown

ACTONINSTITUTE

Christian Social Thought Series
Number 27 • Edited by Kevin Schmiesing

Christian Social Thought Series, Number 27

© 2020 by Acton Institute

Acton Institute
for the Study of Religion and Liberty
All rights reserved.

Cover image: Happy Group of Business People Throw Documents
Source: www.istock.com

ISBN: 978-1-938948-00-8

Interior composition: Judy Schafer
Cover: Peter Ho

ACTON INSTITUTE

98 E. Fulton
Grand Rapids, Michigan 49503
616.454.3080
www.acton.org

Printed in the United States of America

From Michael Szpindor Watson:
To my fiancée Aleksandra Podowska,

*And to Zdzisława Twardak Szpindor (1930–2019),
Robert V. Watson (1922–2009),
and Carolyn Young Lee (1937–2019), in memoriam*

From Grattan Brown:
To Michael Novak, in memoriam

Contents

Introduction		*vii*
I	Wages and Unemployment in the Capitalist Economy	1
II	Catholic Social Teaching and Unemployment	11
III	Revenue Sharing: The Theory	23
IV	Flexible Wages and Economic Solidarity	47
V	A Case Study of Flexible Wages: Singapore	55
VI	Conclusion: Flexible Wages in Defense of "The Permanent Things"	77
References		81
About the Authors		89

Introduction*

> That even more copious and richer benefits may accrue to the family of mankind, two things are especially necessary: *reform of institutions and correction of morals.*[1]
>
> —Pius XI, *Quadragesimo Anno* (1931)

In the summer of 2009, a camping trip brought me close to Elizabethtown, a river town located in Hardin County, southern Illinois. Although my grandma was born in Missouri, her parents returned to Elizabethtown—known as "E'town" to the locals—when she was about ten years old. After earning her teaching certificate, she taught in several Hardin County schools before moving to the Chicago area in her thirties. As a retrophile and romantic for personal histories (and also the one in charge of driving), I coerced my camping troupe to take the ferried route through Elizabethtown. We dropped in on the E'town River Restaurant, a floating eatery on the Ohio River specializing in fried catfish and traditional southern side dishes. For E'town we were exotic: Polish-speaking Americans and

---

* The authors thank Carolyn (nee Young) Lee and her daughter Lazette Bretthorst for their comments and edits.
[1] Pope Pius XI, Encyclical Letter *Quadragesimo Anno* (1931), nos. 77–78, emphasis added. "The Just Wage" is the title of chapter 4 (nos. 65–76) of part 2.

Introduction

immigrants. Curiosity led to conversation with the waitresses. Expecting to find a long-lost relative, I mentioned my grandmother's maiden name, "Young." No one that I spoke with had ever heard of the Young family. The waitresses asked some of the older locals, but no one recalled my grandmother's family name.

My lifelong summer experiences of the Polish countryside in the Voivodeship of Subcarpathia colored my expectations of Elizabethtown. There are just over four hundred people in Laskówka—a comparable size to Elizabethtown. If I were to mention my Babcia's (grandmother on mother's side) maiden name or my Dziadzia's surname there, I would doubtless find a relative or local who could point me in the direction of the log cabin in which my Babcia grew up. There was an obvious contrast between the American small town and the Polish one.

Not wanting to give up too easily, I visited my grandpa, who—just before his sudden death—connected me to my relatives in southern Illinois. I scheduled a trip back to southern Illinois to meet the side of my family I had never known.

I arrived at Walter and Carolyn (Young) Lee's home. Carolyn had been my grandma's favorite niece and maid-of-honor. They lived in Marion, approximately fifty miles northwest of Elizabethtown. In 1955, Walter's work moved them away from Hardin County, and, like most of the family, they never returned. Only the Youngs' extended family still remain around the Hardin County area. Nonetheless, Walter and Carolyn visited often to attend festivals and reunions and eat catfish. Walter was an only child, and the members of his family are buried in Hardin County or have moved elsewhere: Georgia, Idaho, and California. I wondered why my family left Hardin County. I knew why my mother's family had left communist Poland: economic opportunity and their staunchly anticommunist patriotic political attitudes. But what was wrong with Hardin County?

Both Elizabethtown and Hardin County have lost about 50 percent of their population since 1950.[2] Much of the vacant land has been bought by the Shawnee National Forest and will remain vacant as federal lands are rarely privatized. The region is beautiful in its natural endowment, but the beauty of which I was to hear from Walter, Carolyn, and some of their friends was not one focused on nature but on their lived experience when life was good.

Hardin is the least populated county in Illinois and one of its poorest. Albeit culturally and politically southern, it is located in a midwestern and arguably Rust Belt state. Hardin County is more West Virginia than Ohio. The fluorspar mines still operate but they are not thriving. Although Carolyn's father had worked in the mines, he later became a lineman for the Rural Electric Authority (REA). With the decline of the region's mining industry came the downsizing of Hardin County REA. Rather than accepting unemployment and staying near E'town, he moved to Marion, Illinois.

Carolyn and Walter, along with some of their longtime friends, showed me the remains of the house where my grandma had lived and the one-hundred-sixty-acre homestead they once had, which is now mostly owned by the Shawnee National Forest. Near my grandma's childhood home, I met Vernon, a former kindergarten student of my grandmother. He told stories of the old days. From Carolyn, Walter, Vernon, and others I heard of the dire times during the Great Depression and of the good times in the forties and fifties. Hardin County once had good jobs, economically strong families, and a thriving society. Vernon worked in the mines and was quick to mention how trade with Mexico brought cheaper fluorspar into the United States. Carolyn also recounted how the declining mining operations

---

[2] See U.S. Census at https://www.census.gov/prod/www/decennial.html.

directly affected the REA downsizing and her father's transfer to a stronger economic environment.

In 1950 Elizabethtown and the surrounding countryside was a place where children played unsupervised and roamed freely. It was safe, fun, a bit wild, and a true society. In 2009, however, I was repeatedly told by locals that if I were to hike on my great-grandparents' property I should carry a gun because there were a number of drug dealers in the area.

I am a proponent of the free and unhampered market as a means of discovering solutions to the omnipresent problem of scarcity, and at the same time profoundly disturbed by the damage to community that often comes with the creative destruction of the market. When Poland joined the European Union almost everyone in their twenties and thirties left Laskówka for jobs in Western Europe. With trade from Mexico and East Asia came the boarded-up Main Streets and abandoned factories of the Rust Belt. At Belmont Abbey College in North Carolina, my evening introductory economics courses are attended primarily by students over thirty years of age; many of them are from the Rust Belt. They do not want to leave their families and communities behind, but they want jobs and the jobs have moved south—particularly to business-friendly North Carolina.

Why did the jobs disappear? Why did the jobs move to the Sunbelt? We could avoid all the upheaval of creative destruction, but that would mean a static existence with little to no growth and innovation. We could abolish free trade by hiking tariffs and establishing quotas to protect inefficient producers, protect an inefficient regulatory regime, and have American consumers foot the bill. But, apart from serious national security concerns, it is unclear why we should prefer inefficient domestic producers over domestic consumers and foreign producers. Even more, should we protect an inefficient regulatory regime in Pennsylvania from North Carolinian competition? Is there no solution to the upheavals of capitalism?

Grattan and I do not offer a comprehensive solution. We do not attempt to solve every problem with one policy or a package of policies, nor do we believe that market forces provide perfect solutions. Rather we apply sound economic reasoning in a world of second-bests to identify the flexible-wage policy as a means of allowing creative destruction to continue at a human pace without inefficient distortions to the market process that other fiscal and monetary policies incur. Perhaps the Rust Belt need not rust, Ohioans need not leave for North Carolina, and Carolyn's dad need not leave Hardin County.

—Michael V. Szpindor Watson

* * *

Like Michael, I have learned much from my family's history. I have come to appreciate the opportunities provided by four centuries of capitalism in the United States. I can name a relatively few people—my ancestors—who worked in various professions and industries during each of those centuries. In the lives of their families, I recognize the pitfalls as well as the benefits of work, wealth, and poverty. The Catholic intellectual tradition helps me sort through the meaning of those experiences: some explained better by our human condition than by the characteristics and functioning of the capitalist system; others explained better by comparing the capitalist system to its alternatives. Like many others, I think that capitalism is better than those alternatives and that trying to improve its very real deficiencies holds the greatest promise to preserve and expand its benefits and to discover better future alternatives.

Michael's family history tells a familiar story. Families migrate, settle, become unsettled, and resettle in an effort to support and enjoy the "permanent things": loving relationships, friendships, begetting and educating children, worship, shared experiences of beauty in nature and art, and the need to organize work and political activities. A person's knowledge and hopes about these permanent things easily become tied to people and places in the "good times." For this reason, it is particularly unsettling when people die or migrate.

As Michael's family story also shows, economic changes often weigh heavily in the decision to migrate, whether it be to another county, state, or country. Naturally, we search for the causes of economic decline and for the moral and economic principles to spur prosperity. My own family's history tells a different kind of unsettling, that of becoming too settled. Sometimes clinging to the place and sources of economic success undermines the habits and practices enabling that success.

During the nineteenth and twentieth centuries, my family settled and thrived economically in the western part of Tennessee. Josiah Higgason, a physician, migrated from Virginia to Somerville, Tennessee, established a medical practice, and was paid in chickens just as often as he was paid in currency. Yet he was paid. With wealth came leisure and culture. The small family library included the two huge volumes—the Bible and the complete works of Shakespeare—typical of those times. Higgason helped establish the Methodist Church in Somerville, but his true leanings toward Unitarianism are reflected in a philosophical journal he kept. In the 1820s, he had built a large house just off the main square, and this property was handed down through several generations until it was sold in 2002, when no family members remained in Somerville. Economic changes partly explain why no family members remained, but equally important was the social isolation experienced by the last remaining family members, two unmarried sisters who ran an unprofitable fabric shop for decades.

John Ryan, an Irish Catholic, immigrated to Mobile, Alabama, in the 1860s, secured a job with the Mobile & Ohio Railroad, and moved his family up the line to Jackson, Tennessee. Several generations of the family were educated by the Dominican fathers and sisters from Nashville, Tennessee, who established St.

Mary's parish and school, both still growing today. Encouraged by the Dominicans, my grandmother attended Rosary College in Chicago, Illinois, and studied abroad in 1929–1930 at the University of Fribourg, Switzerland. My grandfather, from a Protestant family in Jackson, stood to inherit the family business, a successful wholesale goods distributorship established by his grandfather shortly after the Civil War. Yet he aspired to work in finance and took his bride to Chicago, where he traded commodities for two years. Then, his father prevailed upon him to return to Jackson and run the family business. He was the last family member to do so. His disappointment, and the frustration it caused, only exacerbated my grandfather's propensity for alcohol, and he did not pass on the habits and learning necessary for business leadership and innovation.

The sale of that business nonetheless generated wealth, and my grandmother used part of it to educate her grandchildren, including me. With her help, I was able to study Catholic theology and explore its long tradition of learning about the wise conduct of human activity, including economic activity. In the history of Christian civilization, there are both shining successes and miserable failures to illustrate how certain habits of production, trade, and the use of property support important human aspirations across decades and generations, without undermining the human qualities that make discovery, invention, trade, and sharing wealth possible.

—Grattan Brown

1 Wages and Unemployment in the Capitalist Economy

Michael Novak's seminal *The Spirit of Capitalism* is an apologia for capitalism par excellence. It helped to justify what many Catholics already thought and to convince others: that Catholic social thought could and should explain the positive characteristics and possibilities of the free economy. There has been no dearth of skeptics and opponents of free enterprise in the Catholic intellectual tradition. In the anglophone world, there are the distributists G. K. Chesterton, Hilaire Belloc, and their contemporary admirers. There are the antimodern traditionalists, the devotees of Heinrich Pesch's solidarism, and those sympathetic to progressivism such as New Deal advocate Msgr. John A. Ryan and current advocates of the welfare state. Recently a new group has emerged as some former defenders of the market have grown more doubtful of its beneficence.

Most notable is R. R. Reno of *First Things*, the flagship publication of the intellectual ecumenical conservative alliance. Reno expresses growing skepticism about Novak's relevance to the post-1989 market order. "Today," he writes, "our problems arise from the ubiquity of capitalism."

> The dynamism, velocity, and mobility of capitalism are destabilizing our societies. And this economic volatility seems to be married to a cultural project, one that seeks to free all personal desires from traditional modes of discipline and limitation.

1

> Capitalism has a marvelous capacity to innovate, create wealth, and expand prosperity. But it lacks the capacity to give people stability, solidarity, and a sense of belonging. In fact, in its current form, global capitalism seems positively hostile to these fundamental human needs.[1]

In other words, the free economy lacks room for *the permanent things*, to recall Russell Kirk's use of T. S. Eliot's expression.[2] Families and communities need certainty about the strength of familial and neighborly ties as much as—nay, even more than—they need affordable goods and services. The free economy provides the latter, the argument goes, necessarily at the expense of the former because it produces a society of greater anonymity that undermines familial stability, a sense of belonging, and solidarity within communities.

If a better alternative to capitalism exists, then like early capitalism, let it find some fertile ground to show its human worth and over time bloom in tens, then thousands, then millions and billions of flowers. Then we shall study that future economic system's successes, likely modest, and its failures, hopefully not tragic, and most importantly its superior harmony with those permanent things. As a method of discovery, prudent political solutions capable of directing capitalist hyper-dynamism to the good of those permanent things are more humane than a fearful and pandering political slide into economic "regime-change"—socialism by default—or worse, violence under a cloak of political action.

---

[1] R. R. Reno, "Capitalism Beyond Caricatures," *First Things*, May 18, 2016, https://www.firstthings.com/blogs/firstthoughts/2016/05/capitalism-beyond-caricatures.

[2] Attarian, John, "Russell Kirk's Economics of the Permanent Things," April 1, 1996, Foundation for Economic Education, https://fee.org/articles/russell-kirks-economics-of-the-permanent-things/.

Any economic system must provide employment and avoid unemployment by means that respect the inherent dignity and promote the personal and professional development of the people involved in that economy. It must have mechanisms for making people aware of economic realities such as scarcity, supply and demand, unmet needs and desires, and opportunity, and for responding to changes in those economic realities. Prudent, just employment practices, recognized in public policy, are essential for orienting today's capitalism—or any superior system in the future—to the flourishing of those permanent things.

Wage Flexibility and the Scourge of Unemployment

The central claim of this monograph should find support among most economists, left, center, or right: Wage rigidities cause unemployment. When wages go above the (marginal) productivity of labor, unemployment ensues. The longer it takes for wages to adjust to the productivity of labor, the longer the unemployment will last. In other words, businesses do not hire workers to make losses. Catholic social teaching points to the calamitous effects of unemployment on the person, family, and local community, especially when there is mass unemployment.[3] In response, economic analysis and policy should aim to eliminate causes of unemployment, such as wage rigidities.

---

[3] For example, John Paul II recognizes the corrosive social effect of unemployment as he observes a general social responsibility "*to act against unemployment*, which in all cases is an evil, and which, when it reaches a certain level, can become a real social disaster. It is particularly painful when it especially affects young people, who after appropriate cultural, technical and professional preparation fail to find work, and see their sincere wish to work and their readiness to take on their own responsibility for the economic and social development of the community sadly frustrated." Encyclical Letter *Laborem Exercens* (1981), no. 18.

Any government policies resulting in wage rigidities should be abolished or replaced with policies that increase wage flexibility.

Unemployment is a scourge that public policy should aim at minimizing. Wage flexibility minimizes unemployment by preserving existing jobs during economic downturns and increasing compensation during economic expansion. Thus wage flexibility should be an unabashed aim of public policy. Replacing the current fixed-wage labor market with revenue sharing, profit sharing, or bonus schemes would greatly increase the flexibility of wages.[4]

By wage rigidity, we mean that wages adjust to the marginal product of labor on an annual or longer basis. By wage flexibility, we mean that wages adjust to the marginal product of labor on a semiannual or shorter basis.[5] Flexible wages fluctuate as prices fluctuate, according to the preferences of consumers and the supply of goods and services. When demand increases and prices rise, employers increase product output and thus increase labor input, by hiring more workers and/or increasing wages, in order to increase revenue. When demand decreases and prices fall, employers reduce product output and thus reduce labor input, in order to avoid losses. Or, in economic terms, wages tend to equal the marginal product of labor, which is defined as the increase in revenue if the firm adds another unit of labor—

---

[4] There are many other policy proposals that are complementary to wage flexibility but are beyond the scope of this monograph: for example, policies focused on labor flexibility (reducing the costs of hiring and firing) or that transform unions into recruiting, insurance, and education institutions for labor. Likewise, a Chilean or Singaporean policy on mandated savings, as opposed to government-controlled social security, to provide for retirement could also be complementary.

[5] In some scenarios semiannual may be too long and be considered sticky, especially in cases of sudden and unexpected changes in the economy. "Stickiness" is a relative term.

that is, if it hires another worker.[6] The change in demand for labor—the demand curve for labor—is directly related to the change in demand for the good or service produced by labor.

Wages are not arbitrary but are ultimately based on the demand for products, which determines a firm's demand for labor. The output of labor is sold, either as a capital good or a consumer good, for a price resulting in revenue. The revenue must exceed the cost of production or the firm fails to make a profit. If the product is a capital good, it will be used to produce other goods until a consumer good is produced. When consumers buy a good, the price of that good determines the profitability (or loss) of all the combinations of labor and capital that preceded it. Thus, wages across industries rise and fall with the prices of consumer goods.

If labor is paid above what consumers are willing to pay, then wages are too high. The wages are above the marginal product of labor, and the firm takes on losses. In this case, the firm has two options: reduce wages or fire workers. When wages are rigid, the firm cannot reduce wages, so it must lay off workers to remain viable. If labor is paid below what consumers are willing to pay, then wages are too low. In economic terms, the wage is below the marginal product of labor, and the firm is rewarded with profits. When the firm is rewarded with profits it has three choices: increase wages, hire more workers, or keep the status quo.

If wages are fixed and profits uncertain, firms will manage labor costs by hiring and laying off workers rather than adjusting their wages. They will also hesitate to increase wages in profitable times as they cannot be brought down quickly in bad times. If firms increase (fixed) wages and profits turn to losses, then firms will lay off more workers than they would if wages

---

[6] Some may use the term *marginal revenue productivity theory of wages* rather than *marginal product of labor*.

had not increased. Hiring more employees will be preferred to a general increase in fixed wages, as the new employees can be laid off if profits are fleeting. The absence of fixed-wage increases in good times results in a lower unemployment rate in bad times. Less profits will be shared with labor in good times and the pressure valve to deal with shifting profits and losses will be the unemployment rate.

Some may respond that, rather than arguing for making wages flexible, we should have a fixed wage and rigid labor market, thereby allowing any increases in employment to be permanent. Such policies are often described with phrases like "workers' protections" or "workers' rights." A rigid labor market is where it is costly to hire, lay off, and fire employees. Firms would find it difficult to lay off their new employees when profits turn to losses. Forcing firms to take on losses is a lose-lose scenario. The firms eventually will cease to exist and the jobs will disappear. A fixed wage and rigid labor market give an incentive to firms to increase neither employment nor wages. We end up in the worst of worlds where increases in profits result neither in higher wages nor higher employment. Profits get stashed away, paid out in dividends to owners, or invested in capital formation as it is much easier to "fire" unproductive capital by discarding or selling it. The scenario could result in greater income inequality, which will result in calls for higher taxes on profits and on the rich, leading to less capital formation. As capital augments labor's productivity, a slowdown in capital formation will also slow increases in labor's marginal product. There are no winners.

European countries such as Spain, France, and Italy have historically had both fixed wages and rigid labor markets. The results have been historically high youth unemployment and natural unemployment rates. Countries such as Denmark, Switzerland, the United States, and Singapore have flexible labor markets and have much lower youth unemployment rates and a lower natural unemployment rate.[7] In addition to a flexible labor market, Singapore has flexible wages. Outside of making profits a certainty—an impossibility—flexible wages and flexible labor markets are the best solution. As we will discuss below, the tendency of rigid labor markets and fixed wages to discourage job creation cuts against fundamental principles of Catholic social teaching, especially the common good and solidarity.

There are many ways in which flexible wages could be achieved, such as revenue sharing, profit sharing, bonuses, stock ownership, and employee-sponsored ownership plans (ESOPs). Such revenue sharing may boost employee productivity or may turn the employee market into a "sellers' market" (labor sells its labor to employers), that is, a tight labor market. In a tight labor market, wages tend to increase as employers compete with each other for labor by both hiring new workers and keeping current ones. At some margin, it may be more expensive to increase wages as compared to increasing non-pecuniary benefits. Such non-pecuniary benefits that can be offered to win over labor

---

[7] "Unemployment—Youth Unemployment Rate—OECD Data." *Youth Unemployment Rate*, OECD, data.oecd.org/unemp/youth-unemployment-rate.htm; "Youth Unemployment Rate for Singapore," *FRED*, Federal Reserve Bank of St. Louis, 25 April 2018, fred.stlouisfed.org/series/SLUEM1524ZSSGP; *Employment Flexibility Index 2018 EU and OECD Countries*, Lithuanian Free Market Institute, 2017, en.llri.lt/wp-content/uploads/2017/12/Employment-Flexibility-Index-2018_-LFMI.pdf; Stephen Nickell, "Unemployment and Labor Market Rigidities: Europe versus North America," *Journal of Economic Perspectives* 11, no. 3 (1997): 55–74, http://www.jstor.org/stable/2138184; Horst Siebert, "Labor Market Rigidities: At the Root of Unemployment in Europe," *Journal of Economic Perspectives* 11, no. 3 (1997): 37–54; Alexandru Coita, "Defrosting Italy's Labor Market—Berlusconi, Trade Unions, and the Future of the Bread-Winner Model," *SAIS Europe Journal of Global Affairs*, April 1, 2005, www.saisjournal.org/posts/defrosting-italy%27s-labor-market.

are an appealing working environment, a focus on collegiality, and flexibility in work schedules. In a tight labor market, labor would have more choices: location, income, benefits, and working conditions.[8] More choices for labor means labor wins: Employees can choose where they wish to live, be confident in employment, and seek working conditions that fit their preferences.

The Drawbacks of Other Solutions

Wage flexibility, a microeconomic solution, has rarely been tried. Instead, monetary and fiscal measures—macroeconomic solutions—have been the focus of government policy as it attempts to ameliorate and avoid economic shocks. The negative side effects of such macroeconomic solutions often outweigh the benefits. One approach is to increase the money supply. The new money stokes inflation, which temporarily decreases the purchasing power of money and thus decreases the purchasing power of the wage, pushing the real wage below the productivity of labor. It is a solution that runs out of steam once people recognize that prices are going up and the purchasing power of their wages is going down; labor then demands higher wages. In the short-run, increasing the money supply may also destabilize the financial sector, create asset bubbles, shift wealth to those who receive the newly created money first from those who receive it last,[9]

---

[8] Martin L. Weitzman, *The Share Economy: Conquering Stagflation* (Cambridge, MA: Harvard University Press, 1984), 72–122.

[9] This phenomenon is known as the Cantillon Effect; see Nicolás Cachanosky, "Cantillon Effects and Money Neutrality," American Institute for Economic Research, June 27, 2017, https://www.aier.org/article/sound-money-project/cantillon-effects-and-money-neutrality.

and redistribute wealth from lenders to borrowers, while, in the long-run, it may have no substantial effect at all.[10]

Fiscal solutions to economic shocks, such as increasing government spending on job programs, also have counterproductive side effects. The first problem is the assumption that the government knows how to efficiently use government revenues to decrease the unemployment rate and increase productivity. Even where government spending might be seen as productive, the government's means of amassing income may erode any benefits of government job creation.

Government has three sources of revenue: taxation, borrowing, and monetizing the debt via money creation. Taxation is a disincentive, so if we increase taxes on capital we punish capital investment; if we tax consumption we punish demand; if we tax savings we punish investment; and if we tax incomes we punish labor. Using taxation assumes the legislature knows which taxes will least distort the economy and that the benefits of the government spending will outweigh the costs of the tax.

If government spending is financed by borrowing, thus incurring a budget deficit, then private investment is crowded out as some of the funds that once went into private investment are now invested in government bonds. Consumption spending may also decrease because, with an increase in demand for loanable funds by the government, the interest rate will increase, thereby disincentivizing consumption. Again, we assume politicians and government bureaucrats are able to calculate whether the benefits of government spending outweigh the lost private investment and consumer spending.

---

[10] Jeffrey M. Lacker, "Can Monetary Policy Affect Economic Growth?" Address at Johns Hopkins Carey Business School, February 24, 2016, Federal Reserve Bank of Richmond, https://www.richmondfed.org/press_room/speeches/jeffrey_m_lacker/2016/lacker_speech_20160224.

Finally, government may try to manage economic shocks by monetizing the debt. Here the central bank creates money to buy government debt. This solution avoids crowding out private spending and investment, but it is itself inflationary and thus represents an inflation tax. Wealth is redistributed from taxpayers to the government as the government receives the newly created money before price increases. As the government spends the newly created money, it trickles through the economy, prices are bid up, and the citizenry pay the tax in the form of higher prices. Here again we assume that the central bank authorities, politicians, and government bureaucrats know the tradeoff between inflation and government spending and can fine-tune the cost-benefit tradeoff.

The monetary and fiscal solutions assume government authorities know how much of each solution is needed, that their statistical information is correct and up-to-date, and that the market solution of adjusting prices and wages is slow. But monetary and fiscal solutions are rarely instantaneous, often delayed, and take time to trickle through the economy. In the meantime, prices and wages may have adjusted to the new equilibrium conditions so that fiscal and monetary interventions no longer make sense and will actually disequilibrate the economy, requiring even more price and wage changes.

Fiscal and monetary solutions do not address the true cause of unnecessary unemployment: sticky wages and other labor market rigidities. Rather they provide short-term relief for a chronic illness by throwing costs on the rest of society as if no other solution were possible. Policy should provide long-run solutions when a manifestly long-run solution is available: making wages more flexible. Implicit in this recommendation is awareness that unemployment is a much greater threat to the coherence of the family, local community, and nation, than the threat of shifting incomes. It is better to have flexible wages with low and steady unemployment than inflexible wages with significant and fluctuating unemployment.

II Catholic Social Teaching and Unemployment

High unemployment is not only an economic disaster but also a moral and cultural one. A careful, principled study of economic systems can help communities avoid high unemployment and lessen the hardship of economic shocks.

Catholic social teaching (CST) proposes moral principles by which to evaluate the many social arrangements we find in modern society. Moral principles refer to realities that ought to exist—for example, just relationships—through the deliberate activities of human beings. Because they refer to realities that *ought* to exist, these principles strike our hearts and minds when the goods they protect are eminently present or sorely lacking. For this reason, these moral principles are also useful and necessary *starting points* for evaluating moral excellence and moral compromise in large modern social systems and for recognizing actions that could reinforce positive social structures and reform negative ones.

The most fundamental principles in CST are human dignity, the common good, solidarity, subsidiarity, and social justice. Many people are familiar with them but use them in simplistic ways to attack complex social situations and policies they think unjust; for example, calling capitalism itself a "structure of sin." By contrast, using principles as starting points for evaluating the strengths and weaknesses of an actually existing social system can yield insight into possible improvements to a social system, as some labor laws have achieved, or into reasons why a social system such as communism should be abandoned. No single principle suffices for a complete evaluation, but each sheds particular light on the complex social phenomena of modern economic systems.

The principle of the common good, for example, helps us see the tragedy of unemployment. Most simply put, the common good is a good given to, or established by, a group of people as their cooperative task and for their mutual benefit. People readily think of the natural environment, physical infrastructure, social institutions, and social systems of an entire people or nation as their common good, used for the benefit of each individual and all together. The Second Vatican Council expresses this sense of the common good by defining it as "the sum total of social conditions which allow people, either as groups or as individuals, to reach their fulfilment more fully and more easily."[1] Yet each group within society—families, businesses, corporations, schools, religious communities, for example—has its own particular common good.[2]

Unemployment erodes the spiritual as well as material goods that ought to exist within these groups. Describing the elements that are essential for persons' temporal welfare, Pope Francis includes employment "above all," for "it is through free, creative, participatory and mutually supportive labour that human beings express and enhance the dignity of their lives."[3] The presence of common spiritual and material goods is most readily seen in family life, which CST recognizes as the most fundamental

---

[1] Second Vatican Council, *Gaudium et Spes*, no. 26.

[2] *Compendium of the Social Doctrine of the Church*, no. 165, referencing Pope John XXIII, Encyclical Letter *Pacem in Terris* (1963).

[3] Pope Francis, Apostolic Exhortation *Evangelii Gaudium* (2013), no. 192.

community within society and in which the "permanent things" are cultivated and enjoyed. Catholic tradition recognizes four defining "goods of marriage" that also illustrate the common good par excellence: a lifelong bond, exclusive fidelity, children, and mutual help in developing both spiritual and material well-being.[4] None of these goods would exist if there were not a union of two persons, male and female. None of these goods can be divided and distributed to the spouses. A bond requires two to be bonded. Children come from sexual union. If one spouse is not faithful, fidelity is compromised and trust vanishes. Help is not mutual if it is given but not received or received but not given. Add to these goods of marriage some defining goods of the family, such as care, companionship, challenge, play, and collaboration among siblings and among members of different generations. These goods exist only because at least two people share them. They rise or fall with marital or familial relationships. Each family member contributes to and benefits from them.

It is tempting to say that unemployment affects the family's material well-being most directly, but in fact it affects the spiritual and relational aspects of a family's common good at least as much. Work not only brings the family material resources but also cultivates their spiritual resources, which include the know-how, practices, and virtues needed to flourish as persons and as a family; to appreciate the value of their material resources; and to ensure the wise use of future resources. Work establishes relationships with other families, often through institutions of civil society. It is in fact good that much of this work—the organization of the home; the education of children; and the daily maintenance of physical, psychological, and spiritual health—is not directly remunerated because it more clearly shows the

---

[4] See, for example, *Gaudium et Spes*, nos. 48–49 and Pope Paul VI, Encyclical Letter *Humanae Vitae* (1968), nos. 7–11.

essential character of work as a service to others undertaken voluntarily and motivated by love.

Yet the possibility of gainful employment provides equally indispensable spiritual and material goods. It gives each family member the opportunity to identify needs within a community that they could work to satisfy, to recognize the value of their talents and personal development, and to establish an array of relationships beyond, and for the benefit of, the family. Accepting full-time employment commits all of the employee's work hours (e.g., forty hours/week, fifty weeks/year), skills, and creativity to the goals of a business (or nonprofit, etc.). Fathers and/or mothers making this commitment teach their children about the value and justice of full-time employment, especially if their employers recognize this commitment by paying wages and other compensation that fall within a just range, supporting the basic needs and ordinary activities of the family's life.[5]

A family member might choose to work more than full-time, or to work part-time in order to be free for activities beyond ordinary employment. These choices too can provide important spiritual and material goods. For example, a family member might work longer hours for a period of time to acquire extra income, additional skills, or valuable expertise; or to complete an important, creative, and financially rewarding project. Alternatively, a family member might choose part-time employment in order to devote time to nonremunerated work at home or in other institutions. In either case, that person sets a concrete example for the family of worthwhile values realized through work.

A flourishing economy provides ample opportunities for full- and part-time employment. Unemployment refers to the inability to find employment despite ongoing effective attempts.

---

[5] See also Robert G. Kennedy, "The Practice of Just Compensation," *Journal of Religion and Business Ethics* 1, no. 1 (2010): 8–11.

Unexpected temporary unemployment may provide certain spiritual goods. Unemployment challenges family members to examine themselves, accept vulnerability, adapt their lifestyle, and improve money management skills. It may require workers in the family to expand their skills and strengthen resilience, social relationships, and even character. Unemployment forces family members to examine more closely their community's current economic situation and to consider the needs and desires of their neighbors, or of their national population, or of foreign populations, and thus the potential market relationships into which they could enter. This attention to others encourages the practice of solidarity. Wages provide valuable information for evaluating and realigning economic relationships and thus the practice of prudence in economic judgment. As a kind of price, wages function as signals that inform unemployed or underemployed workers where their labor provides the most valuable service. With the hope of generating jobs in those sectors, businesses seek to realign economic relationships. Thus wages in a market economy can help justify hope that unemployment will promote spiritual maturity, remain temporary, and eventually lead to material well-being.

By contrast, longstanding unemployment and underemployment seriously threaten the spiritual as well as the material well-being of families and communities. In this scenario, economic communities see jobs disappear without hope that their actions can bring back those jobs or create alternatives. In the vocabulary of CST, such unemployment undermines a variety of common goods within family and civil society. Individual laborers lose not only the income from their jobs but also the opportunity those jobs provide to gain the personal experience, know-how, and virtues cultivated through work. Long-term unemployment severely compromises the social relationships that a worker would have had through employment, such as with colleagues, customers, and peers. Similarly, the loss of household income may damage the family's social relationships, especially if the family becomes inordinately dependent for its basic necessities upon extended family, charities, and government welfare. Unemployment seems to increase the incidence of divorce, thus undermining a fundamental common good of the family, the bond of marriage.[6] The loss of income stresses the spouses' ability to provide for themselves and their children, understood in the Catholic tradition as the marital good of mutual help. At the same time, the loss of employment eliminates an important avenue by which parents use examples from their daily lives to educate their children in economics and society. In sum, temporary unemployment may motivate spiritual growth and ultimately strengthen the common good among the members of a family, but prolonged unemployment tends to bring a sense of isolation and inability that undermines both personal wellbeing and the common goods of the family and the community.

---

[6] Current sociological literature finds that, in particular, the husband's loss of employment significantly increases the likelihood of divorce. This finding suggests a more philosophical conclusion: that is, that a husband's longstanding unemployment introduces difficulties that lie beyond the loss of income and include a connection between work and masculine identity. See, for example, Alexandra Killewald, "Money, Work, and Marital Stability: Assessing Change in the Gendered Determinants of Divorce," *American Sociological Review* 81, no. 4 (2016): 696–719, http://www.asanet.org/sites/default/files/attach/journals/aug16asrfeature.pdf; Melissa Ruby Banzhaf, "When It Rains, It Pours: Under What Circumstances Does Job Loss Lead to Divorce," Center for Economic Studies, U.S. Census Bureau, (January 2014), https://www.sole-jole.org/14357.pdf; and Denise Doiron and Silvia Mendolia, "The Impact of Job Loss on Family Dissolution," *Journal of Population Economics* 25, no. 1 (2014): 367–98, http://citeseerx.ist.psu.edu/viewdoc/download?doi=10.1.1.1001.5312&rep=rep1&type=pdf.

Flexible Wages as Just Wages

It is tempting to promise people that they will always have the resources they need and could reasonably want. But such a promise is not true to the human condition, and human effort cannot sustain it. Making such a promise is neither just nor conducive to the sound economic thinking needed to establish justice. Employees and their unions can drift into this temptation by seeking wages without regard to productivity, product demand, their businesses' viability, or economic forces transforming their industry. Business owners can drift into this temptation by seeking ever-increasing profits without regard to increasing compensation for the increasing productivity, skills, and experience of their employees. Communities can drift into this temptation by enjoying the economic stability, social activities, and amenities that their businesses make possible without regard to adverse shifts in the markets of their economic base or to the adverse financial consequences of their governing authority's economic policies. It is one thing to make mistakes in the difficult task of forecasting economic shifts and translating those forecasts into strategic action. It is another to remain willfully blind to the inescapable realities of risk, scarcity, and a shifting economic landscape. The false promise of perpetual resources requires an economic mirage. Scarcity is real.

Inflexible-wage schemes in weakening economies are a sign of this false promise. They enable blindness to diminishing value in the work done or in the goods and services produced, or both. By contrast, flexible-wage schemes make fluctuations in employees' incomes reflect fluctuations in the demand for and quality of the business's goods and services. These wage fluctuations benefit employees, business owners, and public servants because they are more likely to sustain everyone's attention upon the causes of and strategic responses to economic change. They help businesses adapt more successfully to market fluctuations, preserve jobs during economic declines, increase compensation at lower long-term risk during economic upturns, and thus navigate economic transformations in a given community at a more human pace. They help employees judge the value of the skills and experience that they bring to production. For reasons like these, flexible-wage schemes serve justice better than rigid wage schemes.

The just wage principle, as CST explains it, directs us to examine the effects of work contracts on four economic circumstances: the financial stability of the employee's family, the viability of the business, the roles structure of the business, and the economic conditions of the community. This principle holds that a just wage provides a worker the material resources needed to sustain a family without undermining the financial viability of the business. A just wage also accounts for the relative value to the business of the various roles and skills of different employees, compensating productive employees with high-value skills at a higher rate, within a range determined by the market for those skills and experience. Finally, a just wage accounts for the need of local and national economies to sustain and grow employment opportunities.[7]

---

[7] Pope John XXIII, Encyclical Letter *Mater et Magistra* (1961), no. 71, summarizes and develops the previous tradition:

> The remuneration of work is not something that can be left to the laws of the marketplace [or] to the will of the more powerful. It must be determined in accordance with justice and equity; ... workers must be paid a wage which allows them to live a truly human life and to fulfill their family obligations in a worthy manner. Other factors too enter into the assessment of a just wage: the effective contribution which each individual makes to the economic effort, the financial state of the company for which he works, the requirements of the general good of the particular country—having regard especially to the repercussions on the overall employment ... and finally the requirements of the common good of the universal family of nations of every kind, both large and small.

As we show in the Singapore example below, flexible-wage contracts can respond to these four criteria of the just wage principle better than rigid wage contracts. First, flexible-wage contracts assure an annual base salary that the employee's family can count on as long as the employee and business continue the contract. Wages are flexible because they can increase above the base salary by up to 30 percent. Second, the business is better able to remain viable because it can decrease compensation somewhat to address weakened economic conditions in the business, in its industry, or in its local economy. It can also increase compensation when economic conditions improve in order to retain its current employees and compete for new, skillful, and proven workers. Third, the business responds with greater agility to market competition for employees with increasingly valued skills. Moreover, employees are better able to evaluate their skills and seek greater compensation or know where to direct their efforts to acquire new skills. Fourth, wage flexibility enables a community's businesses to moderate the risk of creating new positions and effectively expands employment opportunities throughout the community.[8]

---

[8] These four advantages of flexible as opposed to rigid wage schemes help explain Pope John Paul II's observation that

> the justice of a socioeconomic system and ... its just functioning, deserve ... to be evaluated by the way in which man's work is properly remunerated in the system.... [W]ages, that is to say remuneration for work, are still a practical means whereby the vast majority of people can have access to those goods which are intended for common use: both the goods of nature and manufactured goods.... Hence, in every case, a just wage is the concrete means of verifying the justice of the whole socioeconomic system and, in any case, of checking that it is functioning justly. It is not the only means of checking, but it is a particularly important one and, in a sense, the key means. (*Laborem Exercens*, no. 19)

These four advantages of flexible-wage contracts respect the personal and social dignity of the human person. First, the reliable base salary respects the inherent dignity of the worker and the worker's family, who must rely upon their work and the goods of the earth for their sustenance and who need to plan how to use the fruits of their labors. A wage that fluctuates above the base salary respects the dignity of the employee's performance, which involves such qualities as effort, talent, task complexity, and accumulated experience over time; and levels of professional development, responsibility, and accountability. A fluctuating wage could increase during a period of particularly meritorious performance without committing the employee to sustain that performance at the expense of other long-term responsibilities.

Second, the ability of the business to moderate part of its labor costs respects one of its essential goals: remaining viable during economic contractions with fewer or no layoffs. This viability also respects the workers' inherent dignity because the business continues to provide an opportunity for work and at least a base salary. Third, flexible compensation respects the dignity of human intelligence. Fluctuating compensation may signal workers to seek other skills or employment opportunities and thus informs the professional development of individual workers. Similarly, the more frequent calculation of compensation may prompt owners and managers to shift market position—for example, by expanding operations into new markets, selling off certain operations to refocus on core goods and services or to shift to a new core. The fourth advantage, the business's ability to moderate the risk of creating new positions, respects the need of unemployed workers to enter the labor force.

From the perspective of CST, flexible wages benefit an economy not only by increasing employment but also by increasing economic literacy and awareness within the families, neighborhoods, cities, and industries that constitute an economic and political community. The offer here to market skeptics is that there is a market-based solution to their concern: wage flexibility via revenue sharing schemes. The main source of impermanence in society, unemployment, is minimized by an economic practice that cultivates the most effective and permanent source of economic growth: human know-how and skill applied repeatedly to the practice of foreseeing needs and desires, organizing and using resources, establishing and maintaining just economic relationships, and managing risks.[9]

---

[9] Pope John Paul II, Encyclical Letter *Centesimus Annus* (1991), no. 32.

III   Revenue Sharing: The Theory

The idea of revenue or profit sharing is not new, but the 1984 publication of Martin L. Weitzman's *The Share Economy: Conquering Stagflation* sparked a new and vigorous discussion of its potential benefits. Revenue sharing means that the wage paid to labor is determined, either in whole or in part, by the revenue of the firm. Weitzman's book was praised by such luminaries as Robert M. Solow, James E. Meade, and Paul Samuelson and was called the "best idea since Keynes" by the *New York Times*.[1] Revenue sharing appeals across the political and economic spectrum: to the left because it creates corporate ownership among the working and middle class; to the right because it increases the efficiency of the market process and lessens the need for social welfare and government intervention in the economy. Both Keynesians and free-market economists have endorsed the idea.

---

[1]   "Best Idea Since Keynes," *New York Times*, March 28, 1985, https://www.nytimes.com/1985/03/28/opinion/best-idea-since-keynes-these-are-best-economic-times-for-most-americans-but-what.html. See also "The Editorial Notebook: How to Cut Unemployment without Magic," *New York Times*, April 25, 1985; Martin L. Weitzman, "Business Forum: Wage Rigidity Is the Central Problem," *New York Times*, May 26, 1985; William Diebold, "Cutting the Pie to Make It Bigger," *New York Times*, April 14, 1985.

Some post-Keynesians, however, oppose it. Paul Davidson, for example, contends that a share economy would obliterate capital investment.[2] In one version of revenue sharing where the revenue of the firm is split between labor and management, Weitzman gives the example of 80 percent of revenue going to labor and 20 percent to management and stockholders. Every increase in labor decreases the wage slightly. So if twenty employees generate one million dollars in revenue, each employee makes forty thousand dollars.[3] Holding constant the percentage of revenue, there is no greater cost to hire more labor—the already employed labor takes a cut to their wages whenever another laborer is hired. Imagine the company hired twenty more employees, holding revenue constant: Each laborer would make twenty thousand dollars—down from forty thousand! As there is no greater cost to hiring more labor, but there is a greater cost to buying capital, Davidson argues, capital investment will cease and lead back to a preindustrial sharecrop economy.

An array of absurd assumptions are required for such an objection to hold:

1. There exists severe monopsony power in the labor market; that is, employees cannot exit one firm to seek employment elsewhere, cannot start their own firm, and cannot become self-employed.

2. Current capitalists have a monopoly privilege on the ownership of capital goods; that is, labor can-

---

[2] See Paul Davidson, "The Simple Macroeconomics of a Nonergodic Monetary Economy versus a Share Economy: Is Weitzman's Macroeconomics Too Simple?" *Journal of Post Keynesian Economics* 9, no. 2 (1986): 212–25; "A Giant Step Back to the Preindustrial Age," *New York Times*, April 7, 1985, https://www.nytimes.com/1985/04/07/opinion/l-a-giant-step-back-to-the-preindustrial-age-149542.html.

[3] One million multiplied by .8 divided by 20 equals 40,000.

not become owners of capital, thereby becoming capitalists.
3. There exists massive unemployment or a near unlimited labor supply.
4. Hiring more labor will not bring about diseconomies of scale; that is, "too many cooks in the kitchen." The effect would be a decrease in revenue, so the firm would not hire more labor.
5. Hiring more labor will not increase revenue; that is, the firm faces a perfectly inelastic demand curve, so a drop in price does not increase the quantity sold.
6. Hiring more labor will not bring about economies of scale; that is, more workers increasing the productivity of other workers and of capital.

Manifestly, the dire predictions of Davidson are unlikely and the closest approximation of a share economy, Singapore, has yielded opposite results.

Revenue sharing was popular because it dealt with the controversy of price and wage stickiness. The focus on price and wage flexibility was common before the publication of John Maynard Keynes's *The General Theory* in 1936.[4] From World War II until the 1970s' experience of stagflation, the consensus was Keynesian: a general confidence in fiscal and monetary adjustment to economic cycles. Keynesian theory assumes that prices, especially wages, are sticky or rigid—especially when shifting downward. There is no doubt that union power greatly increased from World War I to the 1950s. Unfortunately, unions historically tend to seek high fixed wages—the main union in Singapore being a notable exception. Unions' desire for high

---

[4] W. H. Hutt, "The Significance of Price Flexibility," *South African Journal of Economics* 22 (1954): 40–41.

fixed wages and rigid labor markets often became public policy, causing downwardly rigid wages.[5] The result was a higher natural unemployment rate, an increase in the unemployment rate for nonunion labor, and *en masse* unemployment in downturns.[6] Without the option of wage adjustment, fiscal and monetary solutions were sought, which famously and disastrously failed in the 1970s, leading to the Thatcher and Reagan revolutions. The disaster of the 1970s and recession of the early 1980s resurrected the traditional pre-Keynesian focus of economists on wage and price flexibility to insure low unemployment and economic growth.

The Austrian economist Thomas C. Rustici argues that pre-Keynesian neoclassical and classical economists saw price flexibility as policy prescription. "For the whole of the Classical tradition," he writes, "anything that created rigidity of prices, wages, and interest was looked upon with great suspicion." Classical economists "rejected price-fixing schemes by government, monopolies in production, labor union cartels, minimum wage laws, etc." because "these types of government induced interventions would make price structures rigid and keep markets from clearing at equilibrium levels. The Classicals *did not assume* that prices were always instantly flexible—they argued that it was *desirable* that they be so."[7]

Thus government policy to encourage price and wage flexibility would align with the classical tradition. However, Rustici[8]

---

[5] Morgan O. Reynolds, "Labor Unions," The Library of Economics and Liberty, www.econlib.org/library/Enc/LaborUnions.html.

[6] To prevent *en masse* unemployment the money supply was increased, thereby increasing prices and preventing dropping wages—i.e., inflation.

[7] Thomas Carl Rustici et al., *Macroeconomics: The Monetary Foundations of the Macroeconomy* (Cognella Academic Publishing, 2015), 353, emphasis in original.

[8] From personal correspondence on the topic.

and other Austrians argue that entrepreneurs would discover and achieve more efficient compensation policies than government policy such as a tax incentive. Our response is that if current fixed wage schemes are more efficient than flexible-wage schemes, then market participants would likely ignore the incentives that the government gives to adopt a flexible-wage scheme. Ludwig von Mises, an unapologetic Austrian free-market economist, in his time advised the Austrian government to avoid taxes, inflationary monetary finance, and government interference in the pricing mechanism.[9] Mises recognized the necessity of government but urged policies that interfered least with the market process given the political climate. Currently in the United States and elsewhere there are many government policies, such as unemployment insurance and welfare, which disincline businesses from adopting flexible wages and incentivize labor not to seek flexible wages to lessen the chance of unemployment. There is no political will to abolish unemployment insurance or scale back welfare programs. Currently taxpayers pick up the bill when labor becomes unemployed; a tax incentive for flexible wages would counter such indirect subsidies for fixed wages and reduce the need for welfare and unemployment insurance.[10]

The *ordoliberals* of Germany, such as Wilhelm Röpke,[11] Walter Eucken, and Aleksander Rüstow, went further than

---

[9] Richard M. Ebeling, *Political Economy, Public Policy and Monetary Economics: Ludwig von Mises and the Austrian Tradition* (London: Routledge, 2013), chap. 5.

[10] Singapore avoided such incentives by never adopting unemployment insurance and by tying their safety-net policies to employment.

[11] Among the ordoliberals Wilhelm Röpke is often classified as an Austrian in his economic theory but an ordoliberal in his political economy. It is sometimes difficult to tell who is an ordoliberal and who is Austrian economist—as opposed to political economist—when examining their economic theoretical approaches alone. The differences between Mises and Röpke are often, for example, related

simply fighting for promarket policies in an interventionist political climate. They advocated the social market economy, which proposed particular limited interventions that kept private property intact and allowed prices to fluctuate freely—the essence of a free market. They believed there were tendencies in a free market that resulted in destruction of tradition, community, and family and so pursued policies designed to limit such tendencies. They aimed at an ordered liberty.[12] Thus we seek to follow the example of Mises and the ordoliberals of defending tradition, family, and community without undermining the market process.

Flexible Wages and Unemployment

Why are price and wage rigidities such a problem? Price and wage rigidities create shortages and surpluses in goods, services, and labor. A shortage of labor drives unemployment below the natural unemployment rate while a surplus of labor causes unemployment above the natural unemployment rate. The natural unemployment rate is a combination of frictional and structural unemployment. Economists recognize four types of unemployment: frictional, structural, seasonal, and cyclical. Frictional unemployment is the period of time between jobs, or the length of time it takes to find a job. Structural unemployment results from technological changes that make skill sets obsolete, laws and regulations that create labor rigidities, the time it takes for labor to relocate, and other factors.

Frictional unemployment is not a serious problem because it is no surprise when people cannot find jobs instantaneously. Moreover, it creates a market for entrepreneurs who provide

---

to their ethical systems and understandings of history rather than their differences in economic theory.

[12] Richard M. Ebeling, *Austrian Economics and the Political Economy of Freedom* (Cheltenham, UK: Edward Elgar, 2003), 231–43.

the service of matching employee and employer. Finally, the period of unemployment carries a personal and social benefit inasmuch as the person seeking employment gains a greater understanding of how his or her personal skills and knowledge benefit others in market exchanges and which additional skills and knowledge might be profitably acquired.

Nor is seasonal unemployment a major problem. Everyone understands that snow plowing is not a summer job; such seasonal unemployment is predictable and is manageable through savings or insurance. Following Frank H. Knight, economists would describe seasonal unemployment as a question of risk: there exist measurable probability distributions regarding seasonal work.[13] Frictional and seasonal unemployment may cause some stress, but they are not grave threats to family, community, and society.

Structural unemployment, in contrast, can be serious, especially when unnecessary and burdensome laws, regulations, and policies create wage and labor rigidities, as there are few (legal) entrepreneurial solutions to such government intervention. Other structural unemployment problems, such as obsolete skill sets, may have entrepreneurial solutions, such as on the job training, schooling, and certificates, while other solutions may be costly and lengthy, such as movements of labor from Ohio to North Carolina.

Cyclical unemployment is also a threat to the permanent things. Business cycles, unlike seasons, are not regular. We can look to the past and make reasonable estimates about future snowfall in Minnesota. In contrast, there is uncertainty to the timing and depth of business cycles, which sectors of the economy will be most affected, and the nature of reactions by governments and central banks. Again, following Frank Knight,

---

[13] See Frank H. Knight, *Risk, Uncertainty and Profit* (Boston: Hougthon Mifflin), 1921.

we may classify particular elements of the business cycle under uncertainty or as non-ergodic: no measurable probability distribution to estimate probabilities of risk. It is difficult, if not impossible, to insure against a business cycle and its effects upon the economy.

A simple reply would be that the best insurance against the unemployment of the business cycle is to save. But save what, how much, and where? Save cash in a typical checking account in a bank? Business cycles are often centered in financial markets. Perhaps invest in real assets and avoid the financial sector. Which real asset? Real estate? Gold bullion? Many assets fluctuate violently in crisis, and government reaction can be extreme: For example, private ownership of gold was outlawed during the Great Depression. Then there is liquidity: Some real assets are difficult to sell and will limit access to cash to pay bills, especially if the economy is experiencing a "liquidity crisis." Perhaps the business cycle is short-lived but is centered in one's own industry and geographical location with long lasting consequences: a large amount of savings is required to survive if you wish to stay in your community. In order to "insure" against such unemployment uncertainty, one's saving would have to be sizeable, diversified, safe, and liquid.

Business cycles are serious threats to the well-being of a community, because there is so much uncertainty surrounding them. Since we have a fixed-wage labor market, when there are shocks in consumer and investment spending wages do not go down with the sudden decrease in spending. Rather unemployment goes up. If wages declined with the decline in revenues of a firm, the rise in unemployment would be much less.[14] As

---

[14] Good fiscal or monetary policy could lessen a business cycle or prevent it altogether, while bad policy may create or worsen a business cycle. While monetary and fiscal policy is important, it is incredibly contentious. Policy changes to encourage price flexibility are usually not contentious.

a result there would be less uncertainty in unemployment during a downturn and, because prices and wages would adjust to market conditions, the downturn would be shorter.

Economists discuss the short-run and the long-run, or disequilibrium and equilibrium. In the short-run, unemployment is above or below the natural unemployment rate. The long-run is when the unemployment rate is near or at the natural unemployment rate. Policy should be oriented at shortening the short-run as much as possible—that is, policies that maximize price, wage, and labor flexibility. When the short-run is lengthened or the economy experiences multiple shocks—as during the Great Depression era—price and wage flexibility becomes ever more important. When the economy is stuck in disequilibrium, there are shortages and surpluses of goods as prices do not move to their market clearing levels. Shortages require increased prices, while surpluses require decreased prices. If prices are not allowed to adjust, markets become paralyzed, and a mild shock may turn into a years-long depression.

With rigid labor markets and sticky wages, entrepreneurs will be wary about hiring more labor in the wake of healthy profits, as labor costs will be fixed and not variable. If profits disappear the losses will be heavier with little room to adapt. Thus sticky and rigid labor markets incentivize entrepreneurs and firms to prefer capital investment—or simply stashing the profits in preparation for a rainy day—over hiring more labor. This scenario increases the structural unemployment rate and thus the natural unemployment rate. Fiscal and monetary interventions take on much greater importance in a world of sticky wages and rigid labor markets—in fact, without markets being able to correct via prices and wage changes, they are necessary. The United States and many other countries have relatively flexible labor markets but sticky wages. Firms do not vary wages to deal with boom and bust; rather they vary employment. The result will be, and has been, significant movements in the unemployment rate. If wages are fixed at boom levels, any employment recovery will be lethargic until firms can match those boom level wages again.[15] Rather than employing at boom level wages, firms will hoard their earnings or invest in capital. Again, monetary and fiscal policies remain vital to recovery in a fixed-wage economy.

When, instead, labor and capital share the burden of the losses via wage changes, firms will fire less and will be able to hire immediately upon recovery, as wages will not be greater than the productivity of labor. Where wages and labor markets are flexible, fiscal and monetary policies lose much of their importance in dealing with business cycles.

A Historical Case of Wage Rigidity

Imagine a scenario of multiple shocks on the economy. Suppose the market experiences a drop in investor confidence and so there is a drop in investor spending evidenced by a stock market crash. As a result it is more difficult and expensive to raise capital and so capital investment declines. Capital-intensive labor and labor involved in raising capital would suffer with either an increase in unemployment *or* a decrease in their wages. Suppose industrial and political leaders are following the underconsumption theory of recessions and announce that wages must not drop so consumption may remain high. Since wages are not allowed to drop with the decrease in profitability of firms, unemployment increases. Otherwise, companies will take on losses and will risk becoming illiquid and insolvent. Becoming illiquid can be alleviated by a loan, but no loan will be made to an insolvent firm by a private institution. Thus dropping revenues with rigid wages and no layoffs will result in losses and an illiquid firm. The illiquid firm will either take a loan or write IOUs to employees, both being liabilities. If continued, the liabilities will be larger

---

[15] It is assumed that firms will be hesitant or unwilling to offer lower wages to new employees as compared to current employees.

than assets and the firm will become insolvent. If practiced across the economy, it is patent why there is a tradeoff between lower wages and unemployment: continuing losses result in insolvency and bankruptcy. Only a government or central bank financed bailout will save an insolvent firm—which, if made an official policy will create moral hazard by socializing losses and privatizing profits. Such a policy would obliterate the prudent incentives of markets where losses punish unproductivity and profits reward productivity.

Now suppose the economy experiences two more shocks: (1) with increasing unemployment there is a decrease in consumer spending; and (2) the government enacts tariffs to protect domestic producers, which ignites a trade war that cuts exports (a decrease in foreign consumption of domestic goods). Demand is decreasing and therefore prices and profitability are also decreasing, further depressing wages *or* increasing unemployment. Finally suppose that the central bank decreases the money supply. A drop in the money supply results in deflation and lower prices, which again decreases profit margins and should result in falling wages *or* increasing unemployment.

Now suppose the government is operating on the assumption that lower wages and prices cause a recession (i.e., an underconsumption theory of recessions). The government enacts legislation to prevent wages from falling. Since drops in prices result in less revenue and profits, the government also enacts minimum price levels for goods and services. The government is hoping that such policies will increase prices and then wages, followed by increased consumption and profitability of firms, thereby ending the recession. The government pursues a policy of price and wage rigidity, rather than a policy of flexible wages and prices. Rigidly high wages and prices create surpluses throughout the economy: surpluses of labor (unemployment) and surpluses of goods and services (unbought goods and services). Firms do not hire labor to take on losses and consumers buy fewer goods and services as increasing prices surpass the falling equilibrium price in the market. If prices dropped, consumers would consume, and the glut of goods and services would disappear. If wages dropped labor would not be fired. Preventing drops in wages and prices, instead, forestalls the recovery and turns a recession into a depression.

The example above is not imaginary; it is a simplification of the Great Depression. The 1929 stock market crash is the investment spending drop, which was followed by a drop in consumer spending. Then President Hoover, operating on the underconsumption theory, demanded that industrial leaders keep wages high. Afterward Hoover increased taxes and signed the Smoot-Hawley Tariff, which pushed the United States into a trade war. President Roosevelt added the force of law to Hoover's price and wage rigidity policies through such legislation as the National Recovery Act. Moreover, the Federal Reserve allowed the money supply to decline by a third, causing deflation and turning an already bad scenario into a calamity. The fear and rumors, which turned out to be true, of FDR taking America off the gold standard or devaluing the US dollar relative to gold, created massive uncertainty before his inauguration, leading to bank runs *en masse*.[16] Collapsing investment spending, consumer spending, and the money supply means a drop in demand. Falling demand normally results in price and wage decreases, but government policy under both presidencies pursued the opposite. The results were devastating.

---

[16] Thomas Carl Rustici, *Lessons from the Great Depression: The Economic Effects of the Smoot-Hawley Act of 1930 and the Beginning of the Great Depression* (Capitalism Works Publishing, 2005), 216–25.

What would have been the result if President Hoover had been the laissez-faire president so often absurdly claimed?[17] Imagine Hoover giving fireside chats over the radio imploring the American people to accept lower wages to save their colleagues from the scourge of unemployment. What if President Hoover called on Congress to exempt flexible wages from income taxes? Or exempted firms from corporate and other taxes if they dropped wages? Surely, wages and prices would have been more flexible and would have adjusted to their new market-clearing levels.

The result of course would have been lower wages and prices. As prices and wages are rarely instantaneously flexible, some unemployment (a surplus of labor) and a surplus of goods and services would come about. There would be a recession as profits turn to losses with a buildup of surpluses of goods and services. Firms must decrease costs to survive. Firms, on Hoover's imaginary implorations, decrease wages paid to employees—a decrease in costs. Labor now has less income to spend on goods and services.[18] If firms do not decrease the prices for their products, there will be even greater surpluses. The firms that reduce prices first will gain the most revenue and with lower wages will discover profits. Firms that have not decreased their prices will lose customers and take steeper losses. If they wish to survive, they will also decrease their prices.

The result is vastly different. In the short-run, with a decrease in demand and no change in prices, there will be a decrease in revenue for firms. Assuming wages move downward before prices, lower (nominal) wages result in less (real) income for

---

[17] The myth is ubiquitous. See, for example, "The Great Depression, 1929–1933— CCEA— Revision 6—GCSE History—BBC Bitesize." BBC News, BBC, www.bbc.com/bitesize/guides/zxy3k2p/revision/6.

[18] Both a fall in wages and a rise in unemployment would negatively affect aggregate demand.

labor and less wealth.[19] Demand would drop further until firms recognize they must drop prices to clear their surpluses. Since wages are flexible, firms will be more willing to drop prices faster and deeper without decreasing employment. The average per-unit cost of production decreases: prices can move much further downward without incurring losses.[20] The firms who drop their prices first will capture market share resulting in profits, higher wages, and attracting labor and capital. Firms that do not adjust will take on losses until they adjust, are eliminated from the market, or are bought by the more successful firms.

As prices drop, bringing about the new long-run equilibrium, (real) incomes will increase. With little change in unemployment, increasing consumption with the dropping of prices, and the normalization of profits amongst firms, investor and consumer confidence would be quick to return, ending the recession.[21] Whether prices or wages move first only matters if there is a significant lag between the movement of one and the

---

[19] *Real wages* (or *real income*) refers to how much can be bought with such income. *Nominal wages* refers to the dollar amount paid, regardless of how much it will buy. So, if prices in the economy decrease by half and one's wage remain the same, then one's real income has doubled while nominal income has remained the same.

[20] Profit equals (P-AC)Q or Price minus Average Cost multiplied by Quantity. AC drops allowing for a steeper drop in P without a loss.

[21] For a similar but not analogous argument, see discussion of the Pigou effect; for example, Brian Snowdon and Howard R. Vane, *Modern Macroeconomics: Its Origins, Development and Current State* (Cheltenham, UK: E. Elgar, 2006), 120–22. The Pigou effect (or wealth effect) argument is negated if prices and wages are sticky. High levels of debt may also dampen the Pigou effect as an unexpected deflation (drop in prices and wages) would increase the real debt owed. Large amounts of outside money (M0 or Monetary Base), on the other hand, would increase the Pigou effect. Weitzman's proposal of revenue sharing would increase

movement of the other. When the lag between price and wage changes is short, the short-run is shortened and prosperity restored.

With flexible wages the Great Depression would not have been a depression, but rather a period of great volatility in prices and wages with small bouts of unemployment. If Hoover's misnomer had been true and he had been a laissez-faire president, perhaps the Smoot-Hawley tariff, the collapse of the money supply,[22] the devaluation of the dollar, the confiscation of citizens' gold holdings, the increases in taxation, and price controls could have been avoided as the crises and spillover crises from Europe would have quickly corrected. No middle-of-the-road price rigidity policies would have been pursued; thus the ratchet effect[23] of permanent increases in government control in reaction to increases in bad government policy would have been avoided. Sound economic policy such as price and wage flexibility prevents crisis from unraveling into disastrous state action after disastrous state action.

Managing the Transition to Flexible Wages

Let us now explore how flexible wages and other complementary policies would help a closed economy transition to an open economy with free trade. Apart from national security concerns,

---

the Pigou effect as would any policy increasing wage and price flexibility. See Weitzman, *Share Economy*, 52–54.

[22] The Federal Reserve was pursuing the Real Bills doctrine where a shrinking economy would result in less money creation and no reaction to a shrinking money supply. See Lawrence H. White, *The Clash of Economic Ideas: The Great Policy Debates and Experiments of the Last Hundred Years* (Cambridge: Cambridge University Press, 2012).

[23] For the ratchet effect, see Robert Higgs, *Crisis and Leviathan: Critical Episodes in the Growth of American Government* (Oakland, CA: Independent Institute, 2012).

it is unclear why we should protect domestic businesses and labor from competition from abroad. Is there not something morally suspicious about subsidizing inefficiency? Yes and no. A strong argument, alluded to earlier, is that, one after the other, entire communities can be ruined without protections from international competition. Policy should promote the good and virtuous society, while not promoting or protecting inefficiency and waste. A seemingly easy solution to eliminating inefficiency and waste is to open borders immediately to free trade, but that would obliterate many communities centered on firms whose methods are now unprofitable. Thus one has to make not only credible commitments to free trade but also credible commitments to a community so that the transition will allow them to adapt.

A principle of protecting and subsidizing noncompetitive firms should invoke much suspicion. If we protect American firms and employees from competition with China, perhaps we should protect Illinois firms from competition with Hoosiers or Pennsylvanian firms from North Carolinian firms? After all, Illinois and Pennsylvania are having trouble competing against Indiana and North Carolina. How about protecting Gary, Indiana from Indianapolis? Where is the line in the sand?

It is different when comparing China and the United States, because Illinois and Indiana have agreed to pursue common goods via the Constitution, whereas China and the United States have some exclusive common goods or fewer shared common goods. Free trade, however, allows China and the United States to cooperate in pursuit of a more limited set of common goods, employment, trade itself, peace, and mutual prosperity.[24]

---

[24] Christopher J. Coyne, *After War: The Political Economy of Exporting Democracy* (Stanford, CA: Stanford Economics and Finance, 2008), 173–94.

If the United States is the entity to engage in trade relations with foreign countries, it should first consider national security concerns regarding a particular trade deal. If it is clear that free or freer trade would not endanger national security, then the prudent pace of making trade less restrictive becomes a primary consideration. One reason is that shock therapy may itself cause unemployment, exacerbating any unemployment already caused by rigid labor markets, and awake a populist backlash. Like tectonic plates in an earthquake, the more rigid the labor market and wage structure in an economy, the greater the disequilibrating shock to the labor market, with unemployment as a major destructive outcome. Highly concentrated unemployment will wreak havoc, thus the US Congress—and any other government—should avoid suddenly shocking labor markets out of their inefficiencies and seek a slower path to capturing the gains of trade.

Free trade encourages each country to specialize in production based on its comparative advantage, which most increases its total productivity and wealth. However, if inefficient firms have long been protected and entire communities have sprung about them, the communities must be protected, which means the transition to free trade should not be sudden; it should be gradual and predictable with complementary policies in eliminating burdensome regulatory, tax, and labor laws. Increasing the flexibility of wages enables wages to drop, firms to compete with the new supply of foreign goods, and unemployment to be recognized and minimized while the community seeks new markets and industries. Rather than having masses of unemployed workers and empty factories creating a deserted town, the factories will continue to produce while owners and workers search for better opportunities.

Say there exists a 20 percent tariff on imported neckties, which makes foreign neckties 5 percent more expensive than domestically produced neckties. In this scenario, foreign neckties are actually 15 percent cheaper than domestic neckties. It is determined that domestic production of neckties is not a national security interest. The tariff is punishing domestic consumers with higher prices and incentivizing labor and capital into inefficient modes of production, thus making foreign producers and domestic consumers poorer. Free trade would enrich domestic consumers and foreign producers and incentivize labor and capital to specialize in their comparative advantage. Once in equilibrium we have a win-win scenario, but what about the disequilibrium? Imagine the tariff is suddenly scrapped and the price drops 15 percent. The ensuing disequilibrium could annihilate domestic necktie producers and throw the domestic industry's workers into unemployment. Communities centered on the necktie industry would suffer enormously.

Now imagine that the tariff is decreased 1 percentage point per year, so that in twenty years there will be no tariff. The government announces and passes the law so everyone knows what to expect. The legislation allows for five years before the tariff reductions begin, eliminates corporate and capital gains taxes associated with necktie production for twenty-five years, and passes a flexible-wage scheme for necktie labor where all nonfixed wages are exempt from income taxes. The legislation would also act as a "bribe" to necktie manufacturing to agree to free trade and as a signal to all other manufacturers opposed to free trade that there are rewards to supporting free trade. The "bribe" is compensation to firms and communities and also makes for compromise between free traders and former protectionists.

The next ten years would be high times for labor and capital, but they know that in five years tariffs will begin decreasing and in ten years foreign necktie production will be competitive with domestic production. Afterward foreign production will be cheaper than domestic and their revenues will decrease slowly for twenty years if they do not adapt. Firms have two choices:

innovate new products and methods of tie production to compete with foreign production or plan for an exit some point after tariff decreases. With high untaxed profits and incomes, firms will have capital to invest in new production methods and prepare for foreign competition. Once the price of neckties begins to decrease, revenues decrease, and firms may decrease wages in order to survive. If a firm does not engage in capital investment and innovation to compete, they will lose 20 percent of revenue with wages following suit.

If a firm decides not to compete with cheapening foreign production, it will pay lower and lower wages, but slowly as the tariff declines. Workers would have the opportunity—many years in fact—to decide whether they will accept lower wages, find new employment, or start their own businesses. Flexible wages coupled with tax incentives and a credible and slow adoption of free trade will give firms time to innovate and labor time to shift into new employment without suffering massive local unemployment. It is a win-win: Consumers enjoy lower prices, foreign producers increase revenues, domestic workers discern their comparative advantage and innovate, and markets equilibrate at a more humane pace. If other firms decide the "bribe" from government is worthy, then more free trade will be possible. Government loses tax revenue, but as fewer workers exit the labor force and require welfare and unemployment insurance government spending will not increase. Government's purpose, in any case, is not to maximize tax revenue but to encourage the free, virtuous, and prosperous society, and in this scenario less government intervention accomplishes just that.

Objections to Flexible Wages

Weitzman argues that a flexible-wage or share economy, when adequately widespread, decreases the natural unemployment rate. His argument assumes that companies will want to hire as much labor as profitable since the wage the firm pays would be shifted downward easily. In a fixed-wage scenario, hiring one employee increases the costs of the firm, whereas in a revenue sharing scenario there is no increase in the cost. Rather, fellow employees experience a decrease in the wage. The firm, thus, has every incentive to increase employment to the maximum.[25]

The first thought for many could be: This is horrible for labor as employers will simply increase their labor force until wages drop to pennies! Such a scenario would only exist if the supply of labor was infinite and labor had no reservation wage, which is the lowest wage labor is willing to accept. No one will work for free. (Laboring for no wage is done either for the accumulation of skills and is thus an internship or is actually not labor, but leisure.) Assuming we do not have an infinite labor supply—though open borders could create an infinite-like supply of labor for some period of time—and there exists a reservation wage, wages will not continually move downward. A flexible-wage market equilibrium, below the fixed-wage equilibrium, will come about. But we are speaking of nominal wages. In the long run, with greater employment of labor, growth will increase and the real wage with it. So, in some short-run transition to a flexible-wage economy we may experience slower nominal wage growth, but in the long run the increase in output will result in increasing real wages.

Flexible wages will lower structural unemployment and frictional unemployment. Frictional unemployment would be lowered because companies on average will be more willing to hire as there is less or no increase in the cost for the firm and, especially, there is little fear about the ability to decrease costs in the future. One source of structural unemployment is from long-run technological shocks where some skillsets become antiquated. In economic terms, technology renders those skill sets relatively unproductive and thus wages decrease or jobs based

---

[25] Weitzman, *Share Economy*, 72–95.

on those skill sets disappear. Where flexible wages exist, such labor will more easily find or keep former employment, resulting in lower unemployment, less cost to government, and more time to search for greater opportunities or gain new skill sets to increase productivity and wages. Thus, flexible wages will soften the shocks that occur when skill sets and experience become antiquated and less productive, lowering structural unemployment. Rather than losing his job and falling on social welfare, the worker has the opportunity to accept a lower income while searching for a new job or gaining new skills.

The argument opposed to the lowering of the natural unemployment rate assumes firms are already entrepreneurial enough to have discovered the optimum compensation system. Thus entrepreneurs will ignore any government policy encouraging flexible wages resulting in no effect. Those opposed to government policy incentivizing flexible wages would prefer policies making labor markets more flexible—for example, hiring/firing should be easy along with low regulatory burdens on employment. The upside of such an argument for flexible wage proponents is that there will be no change if the efficient arrangement already exists, so there is no net harm to allowing employers use of a flexible-wage system. With a flexible-wage system, we either get the same current outcome or a better outcome—a bet with no risks.

A softer argument in favor of flexible wages is that it will encourage higher productivity as employees will be incentivized to increase their productivity so as to increase their wages. Research into the topic has produced mixed results; however, there is a growing consensus, with advocates such as Douglas L. Kruse arguing that profit sharing results in better employee morale, less turnover, and greater employee wealth.[26]

---

[26] Joseph Blasi et al., "Sharing Profits and Ownership with Workers Not Only Make Them Happier, It Benefits the Bottom Line Too,"

An argument based on "efficiency wages," meanwhile, opposes the flexible-wage approach, finding that the promise of high wages in bad times encourages worker loyalty and productivity.[27] Employers as entrepreneurs have an incentive to find the best compensation system to increase the productivity of labor. If fixed wages encourage productivity, then employers will be more hesitant to adopt flexible-wage schemes. Part of the issue may be the culture of a firm or a nation. If employees do not understand how widespread flexible wages could benefit the common good, they may become disgruntled. Public promotion of the benefits of flexible wages is one method of overcoming such reactions. Singapore has engaged in this type of public promotion to prevent efficiency wage affects.[28]

Not all firms will want to embrace flexible wages, even with a tax incentive, nor will all firms wish to pay all their employees flexible wages. A firm that has not produced a single product but is inventing a new product may not have any revenues, apart from venture capital. Employees for such a firm may be paid in two manners: (1) a standard fixed wage, or (2) stockholdings in

---

The Conversation, 30 May 2019, theconversation.com/sharing-profits-and-ownership-with-workers-not-only-make-them-happier-it-benefits-the-bottom-line-too-111803. The authors of this article propose government loans to "employees who want to buy out retiring small business owners." This policy does not increase wage flexibility, and we would not endorse it.

[27] David Levine, "Efficiency Wages in Weitzman's Share Economy," *Industrial Relations*, 28, no. 3 (Fall 1989): 321–34. See also Martin L. Weitzman and Douglas Kruse, "Profit Sharing and Productivity," in *Paying for Productivity: A Look at the Evidence*, ed. Alan S. Blinder (Washington, DC: The Brookings Institution, 1990), 95–140.

[28] Sin-Chet Chua et al., "Efficiency Wage Theory: Evidence for Singapore Manufacturing Sector," *Singapore Economic Review* 59, no. 3 (September 1, 2014): 1–12.

the firm.[29] Ownership of stock is equivalent to a flexible wage as the firm's average costs do not rise with changes in ownership, and once the firm begins making profits employees will be paid in dividends or the value of the stock will increase. When the employee accepts shares of stock, the employee becomes an entrepreneur-capitalist as he shares in bearing profit and loss.[30]

Firms may also wish to use different types of flexible wages and thus any government policy should allow for a wide range of options. Compensation options include bonuses, a percentage of revenue, partial ownership by employees, profit sharing, or a mixture of a fixed-wage and flexible-wage compensation. Singapore encourages this type of flexibility. Some types of flexible wages, such as revenue and profit sharing, require much more accounting transparency between employee and employer while others, such as bonuses, require less. Each firm can judge which kind of flexible-wage scheme works best for its situation and the government should be as accommodating as possible.

---

[29] One could also have merit-based bonus pay, which would be considered a flexible wage.

[30] Murray Rothbard, *Man, Economy, and State* (Auburn, AL: Ludwig von Mises Institute, 2001), chap. 8.

IV Flexible Wages and Economic Solidarity

The just wage principle demonstrates that flexible compensation schemes cultivate economic awareness among the members of society better than do rigid compensation schemes. The just wage principle holds that people should consider the effects of a work contract on the family of the employee, the viability and roles structure of the business, and the local economy. Wages that respond to changes in the local economy by regular short-term fluctuations draw more widespread attention to the causes of those economic fluctuations.

Economic prosperity depends in part on businesses possessing the materials, skills, leadership, and organization to deliver goods and services to a market. Pricing those goods and services requires a sensitive awareness of geographies, consumers, other producers, and time horizons. Moreover, producing those goods and services profitably requires a sensitive awareness of the businesses' most significant costs, which always include paying their employees. Introducing flexibility into monthly or quarterly compensation focuses the attention of more people more often on economic changes and their causes and thus promotes the prudent practice of solidarity.

Catholic social teaching offers several principles to guide the practice of flexible compensation and to show its potential moral value. Solidarity is a form of *caritas* that could also be called "social charity" or a "civilization of love."[1] It is neither charitable giving nor a vague, superficial "I love everybody" attitude, but rather the friendship-like connection of each person to every other person based on their shared humanity and their interrelatedness through social systems. Relationships of solidarity have neither the familiarity and intimacy of family relations and friendship nor the immediacy of obligation to family, neighborhood, town, and city, but they do involve a personal recognition of every person's dignity and a concern for their well-being. People can feel connected to others in this personal-yet-anonymous way because they can recognize the accumulated effects of actions repeated millions of times through modern social structures, including economic transactions in globalized markets. The keynote of solidarity, therefore, is a commitment to understand those structures and act through them to promote the well-being of people whom one never meets but whose dignity one respects and promotes.[2]

In order to practice solidarity, a person develops greater *awareness* about how one person's or organization's actions affect others through the structures of society. In doing so, they become more aware of the relationships of *interdependence* established by those structures. This awareness of interdependence leads to a *commitment* to act through those structures in order to benefit others. Pope John Paul II sketched these parts of solidarity—awareness, interdependence, and commitment—in the encyclical *Sollicitudo Rei Socialis* to investigate the moral quality of globalized international relationships during the Cold War and to conceive of virtuous, cooperative, and effective reform

---

[1] John Paul II, *Centesimus Annus*, no. 10.

[2] *Compendium of the Social Doctrine of the Church*, nos. 192–96, synthesizes magisterial teaching on the concept of solidarity and refers to original magisterial documents.

where political and economic structures had become morally compromised or corrupt.[3]

In this monograph, we apply this concept to local economies that participate in globalized markets. As *caritas* requires prudence to truly benefit the beloved, solidarity requires prudence to benefit the stranger-loved-as-a-friend through social structures. The four criteria of the just wage principle are capable of guiding a prudent analysis of the superior benefits of flexible over rigid wages. The fluctuating portion of a wage offers an economic signal relevant to all four criteria of the just wage principle. The just wage principle holds that a just wage is one that enables workers to provide for their families, that reflects the relative value and responsibilities of employees in various roles, that does not undermine the viability of the business, and that considers seriously the needs of the local economy to create, maintain, and adapt employment and participate in globalized markets.

As an economic signal, flexible wages indicate economic changes more quickly and clearly, a significant advantage in rapidly changing economic environments. In rigid wage schemes, wages typically fluctuate annually or less frequently and signal economic changes by more drastic adjustments, often in the form of layoffs. In flexible schemes, wages fluctuate more frequently—semiannually, quarterly or even monthly—but, depending on the flexible-wage scheme adopted, do so within a limited range. Base pay provides stability so that businesses and especially families can develop financial plans, while more frequent wage fluctuations above base pay signal changes in economic conditions so that businesses and families consider economic changes closer to "real time." As an economic signal, the flexible wage

---

[3] John Paul II, Encyclical Letter *Sollicitudo Rei Socialis* (1987), no. 38. The late pope had in mind the reform of thoroughly corrupt social structures, which he called *structures of sin*, into positive, humane, sustainable social structures, which he called *structures of solidarity*.

is immediately relevant to the employee's household income and the business's balance sheet and therefore highly efficient at communicating important economic information.

To see the impact of fluctuating wages on social awareness, consider who determines how well a business's work contract meets the four just wage criteria. As we discuss below, it is not business owners by themselves, much less government economists, but also employees and their families and members of other institutions in society. Different people might be more attentive to some criteria over others because those criteria more directly impact their financial well-being, but each member of society is influenced by each of the four. Flexible-wage schemes provide more opportunities for more people to recognize and evaluate shifts in markets and the local economy. With a greater awareness of changes in the local economy, people naturally seek to understand the causes of economic conditions, develop action plans to improve those conditions, and seek commitment among a broad group to implement and periodically evaluate those plans.

Families determine what they require to live comfortably and pursue their family goals. Family members are in a position to evaluate not only the needs that they must satisfy and the goals that they choose to pursue, but also the talents, virtues, and skills that each family member should develop in order to flourish as a human being, which includes their contribution to the family's economic well-being. For families in poverty, this evaluation is all too simple. They must figure out how to survive and to increase their earnings, generate savings, and become more self-sufficient. For families moving out of poverty, they must decide how much of their income to give away, to save, and to spend, and then exercise the discipline to follow through on those decisions. The give-save-spend calculus remains fundamentally the same as families increase their wealth, though investment and philanthropic methods of generating and giving wealth, respectively, may become more complex.[4]

Business owners and executives are primarily responsible for determining what the business requires to remain viable, competitive, and profitable. Their task is to take responsibility for the well-being of the entire organization, and for this reason they typically have comprehensive information about the organization. There is, of course, the temptation to use their more comprehensive knowledge to pursue their own interests and unjustly ignore others' interests. At the same time, this division of labor promotes success if some competent, trustworthy members of the organization, typically owners and executives, take responsibility for the whole. The people in those roles must understand the coordinated activities and financial dynamics within the entire business and the social and economic influences upon the business. They develop and adjust strategies to achieve advantage within their industry's market. They evaluate opportunities, pursue the best opportunities by identifying the skills and activities needed to realize them, compete for labor, and exercise leadership by motivating and training their employees. While they should recognize the effects of the business's wage

---

[4] In *Laborem Exercens*, John Paul II sets freedom to carry out the role of motherhood as a moral standard for the functioning of an economy. We argue that flexible wages promote the economic circumstances and awareness for achieving this standard better than do rigid wages. "It will redound to the credit of society to make it possible for a mother—without inhibiting her freedom, without psychological or practical discrimination, and without penalizing her as compared with other women—to devote herself to taking care of her children and educating them in accordance with their needs, which vary with age. Having to abandon these tasks in order to take up paid work outside the home is wrong from the point of view of the good of society and of the family when it contradicts or hinders these primary goals of the mission of a mother." *Laborem Exercens*, no. 19.

contracts on the families of their employees, especially the least paid, they also must recognize and account for the effects of wage contracts on the viability and competitiveness of the business and on the business's ability to attract and retain workers with the skills and experience needed to compete profitably in their market or to strategically reposition the business in the economy.[5]

Public servants have responsibility for an economy (municipal, state, national) as a whole. Guided by the just wage principle, they would try to understand how wage contracts influence unemployment and promote policies that increase employment. They do well to know the community's economic base and the markets in which its mix of businesses participate, and to monitor the effects of policy. At all levels, governing authorities collect data about their community's economy and make it publicly available to help families and businesses to evaluate economic shifts and risks and to make economic decisions, especially decisions about wages and salaries. They would recognize economic and social circumstances that make the poor vulnerable to exploitation.

It is obvious that large industrialized economies hold increased possibilities as well as vulnerabilities for the poor. As a matter of principle, often called the *preferential option for the poor*, CST insists on the need to consider the effects of economic decision making and policy on the poor, who suffer the most during periods of structural and cyclical unemployment. A flexible-wage policy provides relevant information about the value of various jobs, which helps workers earning the lowest wages decide how to direct their talents, skills, time, and energy to increase their income. Wage flexibility provides more accurate information if those at the bottom of the economy can understand, or can

---

[5] The well-known fourth chapter of Pope John Paul II's *Centesimus Annus* provides the best account in CST of the economic and social value brought by entrepreneurs, other business owners, and managers. See especially nos. 32 and 35.

be taught to understand, how to interpret wage fluctuations in a way that is useful to them. In fact, low-wage workers are more sensitive to these fluctuations than any other economic indicator, and thus flexible-wage schemes are more likely than rigid wage economic environments to help them know how to direct their energies, discover a job more easily, and keep the job. This kind of education and practical knowledge enables the poor to participate more actively in the economy in which they find themselves, generate wealth, use it in a manner that helps the poor behind them generate wealth, and participate in democratic institutions that facilitate this process.[6]

Flexible wages promote a more just relationship between entrepreneur-owners and labor by cultivating a more widespread awareness of changing economic conditions, aligned business interests, and entrepreneurial thinking. The last is particularly helpful to the poorest workers, who benefit from greater knowledge about how to participate in a free market economy. A wage is the price of labor, and prices disseminate information about

---

[6] This process illustrates one kind of "struggle against an economic system" recognized by CST, to which might be added the "struggle to maintain just, well-functioning economic systems." See, for example, Pope John Paul II:

> It is right to speak of a struggle against an economic system, if the latter is understood as a method of upholding the absolute predominance of capital, the possession of the means of production and of the land, in contrast to the free and personal nature of human work. In the struggle against such a system, what is being proposed as an alternative is not the socialist system, which in fact turns out to be State capitalism, but rather *a society of free work, of enterprise and of participation.* Such a society is not directed against the market, but demands that the market be appropriately controlled by the forces of society and by the State, so as to guarantee that the basic needs of the whole of society are satisfied. (*Centesimus Annus*, no. 35)

market conditions. All production is sold for a price, and such prices determine wages paid to labor. Thus, when prices decrease and wages do not, the firm—the entrepreneur-capitalist—takes a cut in profit or a loss. Entrepreneurs and firms do not survive by loss, but by profit. If wages cannot be cut, unemployment will be the result. By accepting a flexible-wage regime, laborers transfer some uncertainty about profit and loss from the entrepreneur-capitalist to themselves and in return lower their chance of being unemployed. Put more positively, laborers share in the profits and losses and become labor-entrepreneurs. Their wages and income will vary as the entrepreneur's income varies. They join the owners of capital in the bull market and the bear market. Their economic fates are conjoined in partnership.

V A Case Study of Flexible Wages: Singapore

Singapore's political ideology is communitarian and Confucian.[1] Yet, Singapore, alongside Hong Kong, is routinely rated as the most-free market in the world.[2] How could such collectivist ideologies produce a country resembling the closest thing to laissez-faire in the twenty-first century? The short answer is that sound economic theory is indifferent to the political ends the authorities choose; it is simply a tool for accomplishing particular ends. Often the lessons of economic theory humble the grand designs of political authorities, or explain why the people suffer as politicians doggedly adhere to disastrous means and willfully ignore the laws of supply and demand. Experience shows no shortage of politicians who, ignorant of economic law, ruin their nations' economies and, with ruin all around them, refuse to learn the basic lessons found in any introductory microeconomics textbook. But when authorities adhere to

---

[1] Basu Sharma and Irene Chew, "The Role of Compensation Policies in Singapore's Competitiveness," *Asia Pacific Journal of Human Resources* 30, no. 2 (December 1992): 16.

[2] *Economic Freedom of the World*, Fraser Institute, 2016, www.fraserinstitute.org/economic-freedom/map?geozone=world&year=2016&page=map; "Singapore," *2019 Index of Economic Freedom*, The Heritage Foundation, www.heritage.org/index/country/singapore.

sound economics and apply them in achieving the ends sought by the nation, prosperity results.

Singapore is a case in point. Its political, economic, and business leaders applied sound economic theory to maximize productivity and minimize unemployment while ensuring economic and social stability. Singapore adopted the free market to abolish poverty and achieve Confucian communitarianism. The GDP per capita in 1960 was $427 and in 2017 it was $57,000—an increase of 133 times.[3] Neighboring Malaysia during the same time frame went from $235 to $10,000—growth of 43 times, in line with other East Asian and Pacific economies. When we consider the Price Purchasing Parity (PPP)—what each dollar actually buys—Singapore's GDP per capita is $94,000. The United States' GDP per capita in 1960 was $3,000 and in 2017 it was $60,000.[4] Singapore's GDP per capita in 1960 was 14 percent that of the United States; by 2017 was almost the same—and if we consider living standards, Singapore's GDP per capita is 37 percent higher.[5]

Singapore had many choices to make when it was thrown out of Malaysia and made an independent city-state. There was an organized communist element and some speculated that Singapore would collapse without Malaysia and its traditional entrepôt status in the British empire. As a multiethnic and multilinguistic polity there were many possibilities for violence and conflict. Singapore's unemployment rate reached 14 percent in 1965, with 19 percent of families and 25 percent of individuals

---

[3] USD 2019.

[4] Which is also the USA's GDP per capita when considering Price Purchasing Parity.

[5] "GDP per Capita, PPP (Constant 2011 International $)," Data, The World Bank, data.worldbank.org/indicator/NY.GDP.PCAP.PP.KD?end=2017&locations=MY-SG-US&start=1960.

in poverty.[6,7] Uncertainty reigned, but the leaders of Singapore took action to bring about security and to develop the economy, both domestically and internationally.

Lee Kuan Yew was Prime Minister from 1959 to 1990. His questionable methods of law and justice and authoritarian style notwithstanding, no one can doubt that his decades-long work of growing the Singaporean economy was a success and provides a natural experiment suitable for a case study. Under his government Singapore went, as the title of his book asserts, *From Third World to First*. He began his political career in support of the socialist-style economic planning associated with the Labor Party in the United Kingdom, but he carefully observed the effects of socialism and the welfare state in other countries and foresaw that socialism would wreck the economy of Singapore, a small state with no natural resources and therefore dependent on trade and the creative economic activities of its people. Over time, he moved farther than other national leaders toward a free market orientation. In Lee's own words,

> In Singapore, a society barely above the poverty line, welfarism would have broken and impoverished us. My actions and policies over the last 30 years after 1959, since I was first saddled with responsibility, were dictated by the overriding need that they would work. I have developed a deep aversion to welfarism and social security, because I have seen it sap the dynamism of people to work their best. What we have attempted in Singapore is asset enhancement, not subsidies. We have attempted to give each person enough chips to be able to play at the table of life. This has kept the people self-reliant, keen

---

[6] Lee Kuan Yew, *From Third World to First: The Singapore Story, 1965–2000* (New York: HarperCollins, 2000), 6–7.

[7] W. G. Huff, *The Economic Growth of Singapore: Trade and Development in the Twentieth Century* (Cambridge: Cambridge University Press, 2010), 291.

and strong. Few have wasted their assets at the gaming table. Most have hoarded their growing wealth and have lived better on the interests and dividends they earn.

Lee explained that he later read F. A. Hayek's *The Fatal Conceit*, where he found articulated what he had discovered through his own experience. Hayek "expressed with clarity and authority what I had long felt but was unable to express, namely the unwisdom of powerful intellects, including Albert Einstein, when they believed that a powerful brain can devise a better system and bring about more 'social justice' than what historical evolution, or economic Darwinism, has been able to work out over the centuries."[8]

The disagreeable term *social Darwinism* may come to mind, but that is quickly dismissed once one makes the distinction between the market order where profit and loss determine survival and nonmarket orders such as the family where the gift takes precedence. The family and some other nonmarket social groups are centered around the gift: willing the good of the other, which is the act of love. The market provides the means for the family and community to achieve their ends. When markets are inefficient there is a greater scarcity of means to support the family and community. Economic Darwinism does not imply social Darwinism, as the survival of the fittest is limited to the market order.

What Hayek had in mind is that some types of behavior and organization make sense for a particular time and place and other types of firms and social organizations for other times and places. Profit and loss determine which firms are best organized. Particular types of social organization, like firms,

---

[8] Han Fook Kwang, Warren Fernandez, and Sumiko Tan, *Lee Kuan Yew, the Man and His Ideas* (Singapore: Marshall Cavendish Editions, 2015), 159.

best adapted to the given time survive and replicate, while less adaptive social organizations retreat.

From his Chinese background Lee understood the necessity of the family unit and applied it to every national-linguistic-religious group. Lee's approach reflects truths also recognized in Catholic social teaching such as the family being the foundational community of society. "We live in different concentric circles," he explained. "And your closest circle is your own family, then your extended family, then the clan and then your friends. One is your social, cultural or scholarly pursuits, or sports, recreation and so on. But when it comes to helping family members out, you've got to club together to help your family, because that's part of the culture that you have inherited."[9]

Families naturally found institutions to meet their needs, and forming businesses causes increased economic activity at different levels in society, which provide the sustenance the family requires. The principles of subsidiarity and solidarity guide the relationships among families, institutions of civil society, and society as a whole. Getting these relationships right is difficult in any social system because it requires maintaining just relationships among many different groups in continually changing circumstances. It leaves us grappling with questions such as how to preserve the sacred in a world of dynamic destructive creation. How does one orient economic policy toward growth that strengthens family and community? How could Singapore eliminate poverty, maximize economic growth, and keep the peace?

The risk with destructive creation, entrepreneurship, and the dynamism of the free market, is that many will be unsettled, unemployed for some time period, and disgruntled. If those negatively affected are ignored and marginalized, they seek political solutions, and political solutions to economic problems

---

[9] Kwang, Fernandez, and Tan, *Lee Kuan Yew*, 163.

tend toward increased government intervention and socialism. Singapore has not taken the traditional route in handling the dynamism of capitalism. It does not have social security or unemployment insurance. Rather, the Singaporean government maintains low unemployment with policies that facilitate retraining employees before they are laid off and a responsive market that quickly equilibrates. Rather than having a social security scheme, Singapore mandates that everyone save nearly 30 percent of their earnings in the Central Provident Fund (CPF).[10] Contributions differ according to age and economic conditions and are divided between employer and employee. A part of the contributions is used to buy one's first home, a part for saving for retirement, and a part for health bills—the distribution between the three varies with age.[11] The goal of Singaporean policy is, as much as possible, to make individuals and families self-reliant and resilient in a changing world. Only when the individual and family are incapable does the state come in to support.

---

[10] Goh Keng Swee, *The Practice of Economic Growth*, 2nd ed. (Singapore: Marshall Cavendish Academic, 2004), 53. At times it has been 40 percent and other times below 30. The mandated percentages have changed over the decades. Mandated savings is used by the Singaporean government as a tool to deal with boom and bust. In good times savings are increased and in bad times they are decreased, thus decreasing the cost of employment in bad times and maintaining demand. Note that Keynesians should approve of this policy as a decrease in savings during a recession stabilizes aggregate demand and acts as an "automatic stabilizer."

[11] Lim Chong Yah, "The National Wages Council (NWC) and Macroeconomics Management in Singapore," and Linda Tan Hui Min and Chew Soon Beng, "Healthcare: Containing Cost without Compromising Quality," in *Crisis Management and Public Policy Singapore's Approach to Economic Resilience*, ed. Sng Hui Ying and Wai Mun Chia (Singapore: World Scientific, 2011).

A Case Study of Flexible Wages

Since the 1980s, Singapore has recognized the truth of both the classical and Keynesian schools: sticky wages prevent recovery. Classicals believe wages will equilibrate quickly in a free market, while Keynesians believe wages are inherently sticky and thus government must manipulate spending. While Singapore largely rejected the Keynesian fiscal and monetary solutions, it accepted the Keynesian concern of sticky wages. Therefore, Singapore chose to encourage a flexible-wage scheme in order to bring about quick market equilibration and achieve the aim of classical economics.[12]

The flexible-wage scheme has been voluntary and has undergone improvement. It has grown in acceptance with some 90 percent of firms adopting it and continues to change since it was initiated in the late 1980s.[13] Singapore's policy is voluntary, so companies that will not benefit need not adopt it. Unfortunately, Singapore has recommended a particular flexible-wage scheme rather than let entrepreneurs determine what kind of flexible scheme best suits their particular firm.

Singapore advocates flexible wages with the support of both employer and employee representatives through the National Wages Council (NWC). Founded in 1972, the goal of the NWC was to bring about national harmony on wages and industrial policy. The NWC is based on flexible wages and tripartism: employees, employers, and the government. All members agree to follow the suggestions of the NWC, which are voluntary in order to avoid the divisiveness of majority voting—that is, there is

---

[12] Herbert G. Grubel and Chee Yuen Ng, "Bonus Pay Systems and Wage Flexibility in Singapore," *ASEAN Economic Bulletin* 2, no. 3 (March 1, 1986): 192–93.

[13] Akankasha Dewan, "90% of Singaporeans Were under Flexible Wage Systems in 2015," *Human Resources Online*, 2 June 2016, www.humanresourcesonline.net/90-singaporeans-flexible-wage-systems-2015/.

unanimous consent to the rules and voluntary implementation.[14] Increases and decreases in wages are understood by all groups as achieving low unemployment, maximizing productivity, and promoting the common good. The result has been the elimination of strikes and achievement of industrial harmony.[15]

Every year the NWC makes suggestions on how to adjust wages. If Singapore misreads the economic data and makes a wrong suggestion (wages should go up, when really they should go down), the economic outcome will worsen. The NWC suggestions are not mandated; they are more of a propaganda tool to speed up wage adjustment to market conditions. As Singapore is a small city-state it is much easier for the government to be sensitive to local changes and to consider the implications of particular policies than it would be for the US government. Even if Singapore made improper policy prescriptions, the voluntary nature of the program allows for firms to ignore the bad advice.

Currently, flexible wages refer to a wage that has a fixed portion and a flexible portion. There are two flexible portions: a 10 percent monthly adjustable component, and a 20 percent annually adjustable component. Thus wages can be adjusted downward by 30 percent per year. Since the Financial Crisis of 2008–2009, the NWC has been discerning the possibility of increasing the flexibility of wages by advocating upper-level management salaries be adjustable by 50 percent and middle management have a flexible component making up 40 percent of their wage.[16] For those concerned that such wage schemes

---

[14] For further discussion on the goal of unanimous consent, see James M. Buchanan and Gordon Tullock, *The Calculus of Consent: Logical Foundations of Constitutional Democracy* (Indianapolis: Liberty Fund, 2018.)

[15] Lim Chong Yah, "National Wages Council."

[16] David Wan and Chin Huat Ong, "Compensation Systems in Singapore," *Compensation & Benefits Review* 34, no. 4 (July 2002): 23–32. See also "Singapore Wage Policies," Presentation at

would result in inequality, Singapore's Gini coefficient—a measure of the equality of income distribution—before taxes and transfers is .417 and .356 after taxes and transfers.[17] Singapore's wealth before taxes and transfers is more equally distributed than Sweden, Denmark, the United States, Canada, Japan, Germany, France, and the United Kingdom. Once taxes and transfers are accounted for, however, only the United States and the United Kingdom are less equally distributed.[18] It should be no surprise that Singapore is less unequal before income transfers, as a flexible-wage policy transfers some of the profits of the firm to the employee—some of the uncertainty borne by capital-entrepreneurs is transferred to labor. The dividends of a growing economy are directed to labor via bonus-like increases in the flexible portion of the wage. When labor bears more uncertainty with a variable wage, it receives a greater share of the wealth with low unemployment.

The transfer system (safety net) in Singapore is also quite different in that Singapore aims to avoid employment disincentives and thus has no unemployment insurance. Rather than subsidizing unemployment, Singapore subsidizes employment

---

TUC-AP Regional Conference, http://ntuc.org.sg/wps/wcm/connect/8c914444-0c79-4a7d-8173-3aed3f947662/09APR14+Session5+_+Singapore.pdf?MOD=AJPERES; "Flexible and Performance-Based Wage Systems," STF IR Seminar, Ministry of Manpower, 15 November 2010, https://www.tripartism.sg/assets/files/Archive/Flexible%20and%20Performance-based%20Wage%20System%20-%20STF%20IR%20Seminar%20(15%20Nov%202010).pdf; and "National Wages Council Guidelines, 2017/2018," Ministry of Manpower, https://www.mom.gov.sg/newsroom/press-releases/2017/0531-nwc-guidelines-2017-2018.

[17] Closer to zero means more equal distribution of income, while further away from zero means less equal distribution.

[18] Joanna Seow, "Spotlight on Calculation of Income Inequality," *The Straits Times*, March 20, 2018, http://www.straitstimes.com/singapore/spotlight-on-calculation-of-income-inequality.

with a program based on the United States Earned Income Tax Credit (EITC). Singapore incentivizes lower-income citizens to remain a part of the workforce to gain experience so that they may one day climb the economic ladder of success with a developed resumé. Singapore also wisely rejects price controls, such as the minimum wage with its unintended consequence of unemployment, as a means of alleviating poverty.[19]

Likewise, Singapore recognizes that some unemployment will occur with technological innovation, which may require retraining of employees or the unemployed. In order to prevent long-term unemployment of such workers, Singapore has an ambitious retraining program open to both the employed and unemployed. The employed will acquire more skills to keep their jobs or quickly find new jobs if they are laid off, and the unemployed will spend less time looking for work. One may doubt the government's ability to predict and determine which skills will be useful in the future, so the choices for skill training are largely left up to employer and/or employee.[20] If such programs are successful there will be a reduction in the structural unemployment rate and therefore the natural unemployment rate. The recognition that welfare programs, such as unemployment insurance, lead to more unemployment, less productivity,

---

[19] Josephine Teo, "Opinion: Why There's No Minimum Wage in Singapore," *HRD Asia*, 7 November 2018, www.hcamag.com/asia/news/general/opinion-why-theres-no-minimum-wage-in-singapore/153751.

[20] Chew Soon Beng, "Commentary: Matching Older Workers to Jobs the Key Manpower Challenge for Singapore," *Channel NewsAsia*, 7 June 2018, www.channelnewsasia.com/news/commentary/older-workers-jobs-matching-skillsfuture-key-manpower-challenge-10373304; Joanna Seow and Tham Yuen-C, "Work in Progress: Redesigning Jobs, Retooling Mindsets," *The Straits Times*, February 12, 2018, www.straitstimes.com/singapore/redesigning-jobs-retooling-mindsets.

and social pathologies has led Singapore to focus on adapting their workforce to the incessant change of twenty-first-century capitalism.

Building a Flexible-Wage System

How did Singapore come to such solutions? Obviously the ideology of the government in power matters, but we must also remember that a small open economy such as Singapore is uniquely and disproportionately affected by business cycles, technological changes, and other shocks. Its latitude in monetary and fiscal policy is naturally quite limited and so it has developed microeconomic solutions to macroeconomic problems. Singapore once had labor contracts specifying wages for three to five years—the opposite of flexible wages—and was also on the traditional seniority system whereby stable employment and high wages came with length of employment.[21] When the inflation of the 1970s hit, such contracts meant that employees were becoming poorer in real terms—that is, their take-home pay was losing purchasing power. Fearful of public unrest and of what became known as stagflation, the NWC began tinkering with a flexible-wage policy by increasing CPF contributions and suggesting that wages be increased.[22] The NWC did not embrace the price control schemes implemented by western nations such as the United States.[23]

With the economic crisis in 1985, Singapore began discussion and promotion of a flexible-wage policy where salaries allowed

---

[21] Basu Sharma and Irene Chew, "Role of Compensation Policies," 19.

[22] Singapore was practicing Weitzman's advice before Weitzman had written it.

[23] Lim Chong Yah, "National Wages Council," 9–12.

for an annual 20 percent adjustable component.[24] In 1999, in the midst of the Asian crisis, Singapore decided that a possible twelve-month wait was simply too long and brought about a monthly variable component so that in a single month the wage could be adjusted 10 percent. Thus there is a basic unchangeable wage set at 70 percent of compensation, an annually variable component of 20 percent of compensation, and a monthly variable component of 10 percent.[25] Notice how Singapore recognized the inadequacy of its former policy and moved to a greater embrace of flexible wages. Also notice that such mistakes in policy by governments, such as under- or overestimating, are common phenomena, but unlike many governments Singapore's was quick to react. If Singapore advocated revenue or profit sharing along with its current policy, there would be less need for Singaporean authorities to engage in fine-tuning after every shock.

What are the results of Singapore's approach? It has one of the lowest unemployment rates in the developed world: Since 2010 the unemployment rate has ranged between 1.8 and 2.2 percent.[26] During the 2008–2009 financial crisis, unemployment maxed at 3.3 percent. The highest unemployment since 1990 was 4.8 percent during the SARS crisis. Revenues dropped so much in the tourist sector that even wage adjustments could not save employment in that sector. During the Asian financial crisis unemployment reached a high of 3.4 percent. From 1989

---

[24] Amazingly, Weitzman wrote his book in 1984 and Singapore pursued a flexible-wage policy in 1985. To this day Singapore has probably come closest to Weitzman's policy prescriptions. At least one other author has noticed this as well: Grubel and Ng, "Bonus Pay Systems," 193.

[25] Zongxian Yu and Dianqing Xu, eds., *From Crisis to Recovery East Asia Rising Again?* (Singapore: World Scientific, 2001),157–58.

[26] Unemployment rate for all labor: citizens, residents, and foreign labor.

until the Asian crisis in 1998 the unemployment rate fluctuated between 1.4 and 2 percent.[27] Between 1990 and 2014 the range for the median duration of unemployment for residents in Singapore was between 4 and 12 weeks, while the range for the United States was 4.8 and 25.2 weeks. Since 2009 Singapore's has been consistently at 8 weeks, while the United States peaked at 25.2 weeks in June 2010, fluttered around 20 weeks until October 2012, hit 12.9 weeks in August 2014, and began 2019 around 9 weeks. Singapore's recovery was spectacular, while the United States' was lackluster.[28]

Perhaps one may argue that comparing Singapore and the United States is like comparing apples and oranges. No doubt there are significant differences. However, consider that Singapore's unemployment prior to its implementation of the flexible-wage scheme ranged from 2.5 to 7 percent.[29] Whereas, allowing a time delay for adopting the wage flexibility scheme, unemployment has not gone above 4.8 percent since its implementation. Measured wage flexibility from 1990 to 2015 in Singapore is four times that of the United States, and twice that of the United Kingdom and of Hong Kong SAR.[30] Considering that CPF contributions are reduced by the government during

---

[27] "Singapore Unemployment Rate [1987– 2019]," CEIC, www.ceicdata.com/en/indicator/singapore/unemployment-rate.

[28] "Median Weeks Unemployed [graph]," Federal Reserve Bank of St. Louis, https://fred.stlouisfed.org/series/UEMPMED#0; "Resident Median Duration of Unemployment [chart]," https://data.gov.sg/dataset/resident-median-duration-of-unemployment.

[29] Gavin Peeble and Peter Wilson, *The Singapore Economy* (Cheltenham, UK: Edward Elgar, 1996), 214.

[30] Si Guo, *Price and Wage Flexibility in Hong Kong SAR* (Washington, DC: International Monetary Fund Asia and Pacific Department, 2017), 5.

recessions, wage flexibility must be even higher.[31] Using sophisticated econometric techniques, Rosalind Chew found support for the flexible-wage scheme when she concluded "output is not affected by earnings" and that "the scenario of raising wages at the expense of employment which is seen in some other countries is not present in Singapore."[32] There are no perfect experiments in the social sciences, but such natural experiments as Singapore back up the claim that wage flexibility should be a key component to stable economic growth.

Singapore's Approach to Economic Crisis

Recall how Presidents Hoover and Roosevelt both pursued interventionist policies that made prices and wages more rigid during the Great Depression. Now let us compare Singapore's response to economic crisis. The crisis in the mid-1970s and 1985 occurred before flexible wages were the norm so they will not be analyzed apart from reminding us that the NWC had already focused on bringing down the cost of employment rather than using fiscal or monetary solutions. By the late 1990s, during the Asian financial crisis, flexible wages had become the norm.

In September 1998, the NWC decided the time was ripe to react to the Asian crisis. It decided that production costs should be decreased. The strategy was threefold: cut CPF contribution rates, suggest a cut to the variable wage component, and slash

---

[31] If wage flexibility means the upward or downward shift in labor costs. So, as the marginal product of labor decreases labor costs also decrease. It is also important to remember economic incidence versus legal incidence, that is, *de facto* and *de jure*. CPF contributions may not be legally considered a wage, but in fact they are a form of compensation and a labor cost.

[32] Rosalind Chew, "The National Wages Council and the Wage System in Singapore," in *Wages and Wages Policies: Tripartism in Singapore*, ed. Lim Chong Yah and Rosalind Chew (Singapore: World Scientific, 1999), 239, 244.

government fees and taxes. The employer contribution to the CPF was cut from 20 to 10 percent in 1999 (decreasing labor costs).[33] The variable wage component reduction would occur at the end of the year. The government realized that slashing the CPF, cutting government fees and taxes, and dropping wages took too long; wages remained sticky. Thus a monthly variable component was proposed, but this would not take place until after the crisis had ended. Despite concerns that the cost cutting would take too long, Singapore's suffering was mild, with some literature not even including the country within the scope of the Asian financial crisis. Unemployment jumped from 1.9 percent in the third quarter of 1997 to 4.4 percent a year later.[34] Unemployment in November 1998 had dropped to 3.4 percent, the following year dropped further to 2.4, and by February 2001 was at 1.9.

Singapore's policies reduced unit labor costs by 8 percent from the third quarter of 1998 to the first quarter of 1999 without high unemployment.[35] In the 1985 crisis, unit labor costs were reduced by 17.5 percent between the second quarter of 1985 and the third quarter of 1987, but with a 7 percent unemployment rate and an unemployment rate that remained above 4 percent for three years, from 1985 until 1988.[36] Rather than reducing wages to bring down labor costs during the 1985–1987 crisis, firms reduced costs by layoffs. The flexible-wage and cost-cutting

---

[33] Rosalind Chew, "Global Financial Tsunami: Can the Industrial Relations Mechanism Save Singapore This Time Around?" in *Singapore and Asia: Impact of the Global Financial Tsunami and Other Economic Issues*, ed. Wai Mun Chia and Hui Ying Sng (Singapore: World Scientific, 2010), 67–80.

[34] Lim Chong Yah, "National Wages Council," 13–15.

[35] "Unit Labour Cost Index (Base Year 2010 = 100), Quarterly, (SA)," *Data.gov.sg*, Government of Singapore, data.gov.sg/dataset/unit-labour-cost-index-base-year-2010-100-quarterly-sa.

[36] Peebles and Wilson. *Singapore Economy*, 214.

approach in 1998, in contrast, resulted in a low unemployment rate *and* quick recovery: Singapore's GDP growth rate in 1999 was 7.2 percent and in 2000 was 10.1 percent.[37]

In the early 2000s Singapore dealt with the tech bubble crash, the 9/11 terrorist attacks, and the SARS scare in East Asia. Unemployment soared to 4.8 percent in August 2003, the highest it has ever been in Singapore between 1988 and 2019. By the following September it was down to 3 percent and just before the 2008 bubble burst was at 1.7 percent.[38] In 2004 the CPF was dropped by 3 percent, a much lower number than in 1999. By that time the NWC was implementing the monthly variable component of the flexible-wage scheme. The monthly component is important as we have seen that in both crises the CPF contributions were reduced months after unemployment had spiked and the crisis had begun. The unfortunate lag also plagues the annual variable component as it will be less effective if we must wait a year for wages to adjust downward. Quick adjustments to wages result in quick equilibration of markets, lower unemployment, and quicker recovery.

The greatest test of the Singaporean economy was the 2008–2009 worldwide financial crash. The recession began in the third quarter of 2008, worsened in the fourth quarter, and in the first quarter of 2009 peaked at an 8.8 percent decrease in GDP growth on an annual basis. By the third quarter in 2009 the economy was recovering. As a country heavily dependent on exporting, importing, and the financial sector, the global financial crisis should have severely affected the Singaporean economy. However, unemployment never went above 3.2 percent. How was this achieved?

---

[37] Lim Chong Yah, "National Wages Council," 15.

[38] "Unemployment Topline Indicators, Annual and Quarterly," *Data.gov.sg*, Government of Singapore. This chart was accessed early in 2019 but is no longer available at the Singapore government website.

First, before anyone considered that a crisis was brewing, 84 percent of private sector employees were under a flexible-wage scheme in 2008, and the NWC was pushing for the monthly variable component and warned the labor force to be prepared to slash wages in their 2008 yearly public guidelines.[39] In their 2009 public guidelines they advocated wage freezes or cuts and other cost-cutting measures, concentrating on wage flexibility and productivity improvements. The primary goal was to maintain sustainable employment. They even pushed to "lead by example," meaning that middle and upper management should also take wage cuts as examples of sharing the burden with their employees.[40] The corporate tax was decreased and an income tax rebate was also enacted.[41]

Singapore did engage in stimulus spending financed from its large reserves.[42] The stimulus package was S$20.5 billion made up of cash grants to every employer per Singaporean resident or

---

[39] "National Wages Council (NWC) Guidelines for 2008/2009," Ministry of Manpower Singapore, 16 May 2008, www.mom.gov.sg/newsroom/press-releases/2008/national-wages-council-nwc-guidelines-for-20082009.

[40] "National Wages Council NWC Guidelines for 2008/2009," Ministry of Manpower Singapore, 16 May 2008, www.mom.gov.sg/newsroom/press-releases/2008/national-wages-council-nwc-guidelines-for-20082009.

[41] Rolf Jordan, "Singapore in Its Worst Recession for Years: The Effects of the Current Economic Crisis on the City-State's Economy," *Journal of Current Southeast Asian Affairs* 28, no. 4 (2009): 104–5, http://hup.sub.uni-hamburg.de/giga/jsaa/article/view/172.

[42] John Burton, "Singapore Unveils $13.7bn Stimulus Package," *Financial Times*, January 22, 2009, https://www.ft.com/content/436e792c-e86d-11dd-a4d0-0000779fd2ac; "Government Budget and Fiscal Position, Annual," *Data.gov.sg*, https://data.gov.sg/dataset/government-fiscal-position-annual?view_id=42b84b79-19aa-4681-af29-96bd3e742190&resource_id=98856a60-33cd-482a-9dc4-1ed52e562d5d.

citizen who was employed—a reduction in the cost of labor for the employer. Singapore also augmented wages of the working poor through their Workfare Income Supplement, a scheme that subsidizes (encourages) lower income labor to work.[43] Other moves made by the government were to set aside money for the financial sector, delay and defer payment on particular bills for taxpayers, a 40 percent property tax rebate, and S$4.4 billion of spending on infrastructure, education, and hospitals.[44] During recessions Singapore also restricts immigration to decrease the unemployment rate.[45]

Low unemployment was the result despite a massive decrease in GDP. Unit labor costs decreased from the end of 2008 to 2010 by 12 percent.[46] From 2009 until 2010 monthly nominal wages dropped between 4.6 and 1.3 percent on an annual basis per quarter.[47] In 2009 the median duration of unemployment was ten months, but dropped to eight months in 2010 and has remained there.[48] In 2010 Singapore's economy grew by 15.24 percent, 6.35 percent the year after, and between 2.2 and 5.11

---

[43] Rosalind Chew, "Global Financial Tsunami," 67–80.

[44] "Jobs Credit Scheme and Budget 2009 Tax Rebates," *Jobs Credit Scheme and Budget 2009 Tax Rebates*, Inland Revenue Authority of Singapore, www.iras.gov.sg/irashome/News-and-Events/Newsroom/Media-Releases-and-Speeches/Media-Releases/2009/Jobs-Credit-Scheme-and-Budget-2009-Tax-Rebates/.

[45] Rolf Jordan, "Singapore in Its Worst Recession," 104–6.

[46] "Unit Labour Cost Index (Base Year 2015 = 100), Quarterly, (SA)," *Data.gov.sg*, https://data.gov.sg/dataset/nit-labour-cost-index-base-year-2015-100-quarterly-sa.

[47] "Year-On-Year Change (%) in Average Monthly Nominal Earnings Per Employee, Quarterly," *Data.gov.sg*, data.gov.sg/dataset/changes-in-average-monthly-nominal-earnings-per-employee-quarterly.

[48] The most recent data available as of early 2019 is up to 2015. "Resident Median Duration of Unemployment," Data.gov.sg, data.gov.sg/dataset/resident-median-duration-of-unemployment?view

A Case Study of Flexible Wages

percent the following years. One would expect a massive drop in GDP during the 2008–2009 financial meltdown to justify such growth; however, in 2008 the growth rate was 1.8 percent and in 2009 the growth rate was -0.6.[49] Perhaps being the most-free market country in the world with flexible prices and wages and policies focused on decreasing the costs of labor has resulted in a growth and recovery miracle.

Compare the propaganda in Singapore to Presidents Hoover and Roosevelt. Singapore rejects the underconsumption theory of recessions and does not seek high wages but high productivity: It recognizes that wages are a function of production.[50] Where Hoover demanded high wages be paid by upper management to labor, Singapore suggests that management act in solidarity with labor by sharing in the pain of wage cuts. Where FDR (and Hoover) pursued policies of controlling prices, cartelizing industry, funding public work projects, raising taxes, and shutting down trade, Singapore focused on market equilibration and productivity to achieve the same ends. Singapore succeeded while Hoover and FDR led us into the Great Depression.

If the United States would have followed Singapore's example in the 2008–2009 financial crisis, the United States would have

---

_id=00ee3324-fe78-4430-b9ee-3b7f2ede1e44&resource_id=2b7fd879-8601-41cd-8bda-2821f9857d2f.

[49] "GDP Growth (Annual %)," Data, The World Bank, data.worldbank.org/indicator/NY.GDP.MKTP.KD.ZG?locations=SG.

[50] Also known as Say's Law. Named after economist J. B. Say, Say's law states that we produce to consume, not consume to produce. We produce so we may consume the production of others through trade. John Maynard Keynes mistakenly believed that Say's law claimed that supply creates its own demand. But the idea behind Say's law is that production allows for consumption and relies on a market with flexible prices. With sticky prices and wages Say's law is less applicable, as markets lag in equilibrating.

enacted the following policies (excluding monetary policy, which is beyond the scope of this discussion):

1. Already having in place a flexible-wage policy, during the crisis the government would have pleaded for employers to cut labor costs and wages to prevent unemployment.
2. It would have abolished or lessened FICA taxes until the recession ended. This would have mimicked the reduction in CPF contributions that Singapore practices. If FICA taxes had been abolished this would have been equivalent to a 7.65 percent decrease in labor costs and an equal increase in post-tax wages.[51]
3. It would have given a monthly tax credit to all employers per full-time employee.[52]
4. It would have lowered the corporate tax rate and other fees and taxes on businesses.

Policies 2–4 could easily be enacted, but the policy of having flexible wages is not something that can be enacted and accepted overnight. It takes time for the policy to be adopted by firms

---

[51] FICA taxes are paid by both employer and employee and when added together equal 15.3 percent of incomes up to some maximum. The reduction of labor costs would only occur in the short run, during the recession and/or the time period for wages to increase as employers bid up wages from the increase in their revenue. Or in economic jargon: Economic incidence is determined by the elasticities of demand and supply.

[52] For those nervous about fiscal deficits, consider that, in the United States, the unemployed take unemployment insurance and often take welfare. Such a tax credit would lessen the increase of welfare and unemployment insurance recipients and prevent a drop in production.

and for experimentation to discover what kind of flexible-wage policies are most efficient.

The United States would not be able to perfectly imitate Singapore, as Singapore is a tiny city-state. The United States does not have the ability to monitor and fine-tune economic policy as closely as Singapore. Thus the United States must choose a policy that incentivizes firms to adopt some flexible-wage policy, while not specifying which flexible scheme is best. Some economists have endorsed a tax incentive to encourage adoption and pay for the possible higher costs of implementing a flexible wage.[53]

How should the United States pursue a flexible-wage policy? First, the government should not choose what kind of flexible-wage scheme should be enacted. Second, the tax incentive should be open to all flexible-wage schemes. Third, any policy should overestimate the need for flexible wages, rather than underestimate. There are no downsides to overestimating, apart from lower tax revenues for the government, but if we underestimate the need for flexible wages we achieve little benefit. A variety of tax incentives could be enacted, such as: (1) lessen or abolish income taxes on flexible wages; (2) enact a tax credit for employees and employers based on what proportion of the wage is flexible; (3) abolish or lessen corporate taxes for firms with flexible wages; or, (4) classify flexible wages as dividend income taxed at the long-run capital gains tax rate, exempt from income and FICA taxes. A possibly significant barrier for flexible wages is the existence of unemployment insurance: If a flexible wage decreased to $500 a week and an unemployment benefit paid $450 a week, many employees would prefer to be laid off than take a wage cut. To avoid that scenario, unemployment benefits

---

[53] Daniel J. B. Mitchell, "Profit Sharing and Employee Ownership: Policy Implications," *Contemporary Economic Policy* 13, no. 2 (April 1995): 16.

should be abolished, shortened, or should be made a function of the fixed portion of a wage.

If such policies lessen cyclical and structural unemployment, the policies could very well pay for themselves as fewer people accept welfare and unemployment insurance and more people are employed, paying taxes and increasing production. The political need for countercyclical fiscal and monetary policies will decrease as will government programs financially supporting the poor. Families and communities will be resilient, subsidiarity will thrive, and the need and desire for the government to intervene will pass.

VI Conclusion: Flexible Wages in Defense of "The Permanent Things"

The notion that there must be a trade-off between thriving communities and the free economy is false. The dynamism of creative destruction inherent to capitalism is not entirely, even mostly, to blame for the displacement of labor and loss of community. Some blame must be cast on our adherence to fixed-wage schemes, their unrealistic assumptions about ongoing economic growth, and their consequent inability to adapt to economic shifts. The true tradeoff is not between stagnation with stable employment or growth with labor displacement, but between variable wages or variable employment. We learn several things from our case study of Singapore, the only country with a widespread flexible-wage policy: (1) the natural unemployment rate decreased, (2) the average length of unemployment decreased, and (3) movements around the natural unemployment rate from economic shocks significantly lessened. Greater dynamism in wages stabilizes employment and counters the greatest economic threat to any community: prolonged, structural unemployment. Wage flexibility protects employment and facilitates adjustments in the allocation of labor at a humane pace. Policies encouraging fixed wages and rigid labor markets should be abolished, and policies encouraging flexible wages enacted.

Flexible-wage practices not only rest on sound economic principles but also promote the virtues of wise reflection on actual economic conditions and of prudent economic decision making within the firm and the family. The principles of Catholic social teaching spotlight these virtues and thus these practices. The just wage principle directs us to examine the effects of work contracts on the well-being of the employee's family, the viability of the business, the varied contributions of different employees to the business, and the needs of the local economy, especially for job creation. Flexible wages provide essential economic information for employers and employees to examine these effects upon the families of employees and owners, and indirectly upon the local economy. People in different roles, employee or employer, might take more responsibility for a particular criterion of the just wage principle: effect on family income and on the viability of the business, respectively. Yet persons in each role give attention to each criterion by the virtues of justice and solidarity. In particular, solidarity disposes people to act in ways that, in this case, avoid unemployment while recognizing the reality of economic uncertainty. Greater flexibility in wages means broader sharing—a hallmark of solidarity—of both risk and reward among employees and employers.

When entrepreneurs share the profits (and losses) with labor, they transfer some of the uncertainty to labor. Entrepreneurs will be more motivated to hire labor during periods of expansion because flexible wages will enable them to manage labor costs during periods of contraction. Entrepreneurs will be more willing to share profits with labor since those higher wages are not permanent wage increases. Thus unemployment is lessened in times of growth *and* recession. Less unemployment and more stable employment benefit communities with greater economic growth and less reliance on government aid, benefit laborers with more choice in employment, and benefit families with more secure long-term income.

A family income represents its material well-being—and much more. It represents a part of the value of a family member's work. Whether remunerated or not, work is an opportunity for personal and professional development and may even become an aspect of personal identity. Moreover, the opportunity to work outside the home brings important social connections and learning to each member of the family. Supported by the opportunity to work and the fruits of the family members' labors, the family itself most securely connects its individual members to the more long-lasting—and in some respects permanent—goods of human existence: intimate relationship, friendship, strength of character, accumulated, prudently managed wealth, and transcendent and religious realities. For this reason, social science and CST agree that the family is the fundamental community within society. Thus we illustrate the destructive effects of unemployment and the motivating possibilities of economic change in terms of the common goods of the family: the bond between the spouses, their fidelity and exclusive intimacy, the conception and education of their children, and mutual help among all the members of the family. The market is where families and communities provide people with the means to seek and pursue the varied goals of a good life.

The great classical economists demonstrated the necessity of free and flexible wages to any functioning, equilibrating market. Keynesians assume the inherent rigidity of wages, which leads to high unemployment, economic depression, and chronic disequilibrium. But the Keynesian assumption of rigid wages is null with flexible-wage policies. Widespread flexible-wage schemes in a market system enable economic adjustments necessary in any economy, as classical economic theory demonstrates. Thus, flexible-wage policy should be agreeable to both classicals and Keynesians.

Revenue sharing, profit sharing, and other flexible-wage schemes should also be attractive across the political spectrum: The noncommunist, nonsocialist left, progressive liberals, centrists, classical liberals, laissez-faire free marketeers, traditionalists, distributists, conservatives, libertarians, and nationalists should all see the benefits of exiting the fixed-wage regime. The left will see it as labor becoming the co-owners of capital, ameliorating the capitalist-labor class divide. Libertarians and conservatives will embrace the waning demand for government aid and services and the increase in local governance. Social conservatives will appreciate the effects of stable employment and lower structural unemployment on the overall well-being of the family.

We have proposed *a* solution—not *the* solution—to the disturbances of modern capitalist regimes discussed by critics such as R. R. Reno. Our solution does not oppose or undermine the foundations of a free economy: private property, the freedom to exchange, the existence of sound money, or the free formation of prices. Rather we seek to defend and strengthen the free formation of prices, specifically the price of labor (the wage), in service of family and community.

References

Church Documents

All documents are available at www.vatican.va.

Pope Francis, Apostolic Exhortation *Evangelii Gaudium* (2013).

Pontifical Council for Justice and Peace, *Compendium of the Social Doctrine of the Church* (2004).

Pope John Paul II, Encyclical Letter *Centesimus Annus* (1991).

Pope John Paul II, Encyclical Letter *Sollicitudo Rei Socialis* (1987).

Pope John Paul II, Encyclical Letter *Laborem Exercens* (1981).

Pope Paul VI, Encyclical Letter *Humanae Vitae* (1968).

Second Vatican Council, *Gaudium et Spes* (Pastoral Constitution on the Church in the Modern World, 1965).

Pope John XXIII, Encyclical Letter *Mater et Magistra* (1961).

Pope Pope Pius XI, Encyclical Letter *Quadragesimo Anno* (1931).

References

Other Sources

In addition to the following, many data were retrieved from online government reports in the United States and Singapore; the sources for those data can be found in the footnotes.

Attarian, John. "Russell Kirk's Economics of the Permanent Things." Foundation for Economic Education, April 1, 1996, https://fee.org/articles/russell-kirks-economics-of-the-permanent-things/.

Banzhaf, Melissa Ruby. "When It Rains, It Pours: Under What Circumstances Does Job Loss Lead to Divorce." Center for Economic Studies, U.S. Census Bureau, January 2014, https://www.sole-jole.org/14357.pdf.

Blasi, Joseph et al. "Sharing Profits and Ownership with Workers Not Only Make Them Happier, It Benefits the Bottom Line Too." *The Conversation*, May 30, 2019, https://www.theconversation.com/sharing-profits-and-ownership-with-workers-not-only-make-them-happier-it-benefits-the-bottom-line-too-111803.

Buchanan, James M., and Gordon Tullock. *The Calculus of Consent: Logical Foundations of Constitutional Democracy*. Indianapolis: Liberty Fund, 2018.

Burton, John. "Singapore Unveils $13.7bn Stimulus Package." *Financial Times*, January 22, 2009, https://www.ft.com/content/436e792c-e86d-11dd-a4d0-0000779fd2ac.

Cachanosky, Nicolás. "Cantillon Effects and Money Neutrality." American Institute for Economic Research, June 27, 2017, https://www.aier.org/article/sound-money-project/cantillon-effects-and-money-neutrality.

Chew, Rosalind. "Global Financial Tsunami: Can the Industrial Relations Mechanism Save Singapore This Time Around?" In *Singapore and Asia: Impact of the Global Financial Tsunami and Other Economic Issues*. Edited by Wai Mun Chia and Hui Ying Sng. Singapore: World Scientific, 2010.

References

Chew, Rosalind. "The National Wages Council and the Wage System in Singapore." In *Wages and Wages Policies: Tripartism in Singapore*. Edited by Lim Chong Yah and Rosalind Chew. Singapore: World Scientific, 1999.

Chew Soon Beng. "Commentary: Matching Older Workers to Jobs the Key Manpower Challenge for Singapore." CNA, 8 June 2018, www.channelnewsasia.com/news/commentary/older-workers-jobs-matching-skillsfuture-key-manpower-challenge-10373304.

Chua, Sin-Chet et al. "Efficiency Wage Theory: Evidence for Singapore Manufacturing Sector." *Singapore Economic Review* 59, no. 3 (2014): 1–12.

Coita, Alexandru. "Defrosting Italy's Labor Market—Berlusconi, Trade Unions, and the Future of the Bread-Winner Model." *SAIS Europe Journal of Global Affairs*, April 1, 2005, www.saisjournal.org/posts/defrosting-italy%27s-labor-market.

Coyne, Christopher J. *After War: The Political Economy of Exporting Democracy*. Stanford: Stanford University Press, 2008.

Davidson, Paul. "The Simple Macroeconomics of a Nonergodic Monetary Economy versus a Share Economy: Is Weitzman's Macroeconomics Too Simple?" *Journal of Post Keynesian Economics* 9, no. 2 (1986): 212–25.

Dewan, Akankasha. "90% of Singaporeans Were under Flexible Wage Systems in 2015." *Human Resources Online*, 2 June 2016, www.humanresourcesonline.net/90-singaporeans-flexible-wage-systems-2015/.

Diebold, William. "Cutting the Pie to Make It Bigger." *New York Times*, April 14, 1985.

Doiron, Denise, and Silvia Mendolia. "The Impact of Job Loss on Family Dissolution." *Journal of Population Economics* 25, no. 1 (2014): 367–98, http://citeseerx.ist.psu.edu/viewdoc/download?doi=10.1.1.1001.5312&rep=rep1&type=pdf.

Ebeling, Richard M. *Austrian Economics and the Political Economy of Freedom*. Cheltenham, UK: Edward Elgar, 2003.

References

Ebeling, Richard M. *Political Economy, Public Policy and Monetary Economics: Ludwig Von Mises and the Austrian Tradition*. London: Routledge, 2013.

Economic Freedom of the World. Fraser Institute, 2016, www.fraser-institute.org/economic-freedom/map?geozone=world&year=2016&page=map.

Employment Flexibility Index, 2018 EU and OECD Countries. Lithuanian Free Market Institute, 2017, en.llri.lt/wp-content/uploads/2017/12/Employment-Flexibility-Index-2018_-LFMI.pdf.

Goh Keng Swee. *The Practice of Economic Growth*, 2nd ed. Singapore: Marshall Cavendish Academic, 2004.

Grubel, Herbert G., and Chee Yuen Ng. "Bonus Pay Systems and Wage Flexibility in Singapore." *ASEAN Economic Bulletin* 2, no. 3 (March 1, 1986): 186–95.

Han Fook Kwang, Warren Fernandez, and Sumiko Tan. *Lee Kuan Yew, the Man and His Ideas*. Singapore: Marshall Cavendish Editions, 2015.

Higgs, Robert. *Crisis and Leviathan: Critical Episodes in the Growth of American Government*. Oakland, CA: Independent Institute, 2012.

Huff, W. G. *The Economic Growth of Singapore: Trade and Development in the Twentieth Century*. Cambridge: Cambridge University Press, 2010.

Hutt, W. H. "The Significance of Price Flexibility." *South African Journal of Economics*, 22 (1954): 40–51.

Jordan, Rolf. "Singapore in Its Worst Recession for Years: The Effects of the Current Economic Crisis on the City-State's Economy." *Journal of Current Southeast Asian Affairs* 28, no. 4 (2009): 95–110, http://hup.sub.uni-hamburg.de/giga/jsaa/article/view/172.

Kennedy, Robert G. "The Practice of Just Compensation." *Journal of Religion and Business Ethics* 1, no. 1 (2010), 1–17.

References

Killewald, Alexandra. "Money, Work, and Marital Stability: Assessing Change in Gendered Determinants of Divorce." *American Sociological Review* 81, no. 4 (2016): 696–719.

Knight, Frank H. *Risk, Uncertainty and Profit*. Boston: Houghton Mifflin, 1921.

Lacker, Jeffrey M. "Can Monetary Policy Affect Economic Growth?" Address at Johns Hopkins Carey Business School, February 24, 2016. Federal Reserve Bank of Richmond, https://www.richmondfed.org/press_room/speeches/jeffrey_m_lacker/2016/lacker_speech_20160224.

Lee Kuan Yew. *From Third World to First: The Singapore Story, 1965–2000*. New York: HarperCollins, 2000.

Levine, David. "Efficiency Wages in Weitzman's Share Economy." *Industrial Relations* 28, no. 3 (Fall 1989): 321–34.

Lim Chong Yah. "The National Wages Council (NWC) and Macroeconomics Management in Singapore." In *Crisis Management and Public Policy Singapore's Approach to Economic Resilience*. Edited by Sng Hui Ying and Wai Mun Chia. Singapore: World Scientific, 2011.

Min, Linda Tan Hui, and Chew Soon Beng. "Healthcare: Containing Cost Without Compromising Quality." In *Crisis Management and Public Policy Singapore's Approach to Economic Resilience*. Edited by Sng Hui Ying and Wai Mun Chia. Singapore: World Scientific, 2011.

Mitchell, Daniel J. B. "Profit Sharing and Employee Ownership: Policy Implications." *Contemporary Economic Policy* 13, no. 2 (April 1995): 16–25.

Nickell, Stephen. "Unemployment and Labor Market Rigidities: Europe versus North America." *The Journal of Economic Perspectives* 11, no. 3 (1997): 55–74.

Peebles, Gavin, and Peter Wilson. *The Singapore Economy*. Cheltenham, UK: Edward Elgar, 1996.

References

Reno, R. R. "Capitalism Beyond Caricatures." *First Things*, May 18, 2016, https://www.firstthings.com/blogs/firstthoughts/2016/05/capitalism-beyond-caricatures.

Reynolds, Morgan O. "Labor Unions." The Library of Economics and Liberty, www.econlib.org/library/Enc/LaborUnions.html.

Rothbard, Murray. *Man, Economy, and State*. Auburn, AL: Ludwig von Mises Institute, 2001.

Rustici, Thomas Carl et al. *Macroeconomics: The Monetary Foundations of the Macroeconomy*. San Diego: Cognella Academic, 2015.

Rustici, Thomas Carl. *Lessons from the Great Depression: The Economic Effects of the Smoot-Hawley Act of 1930 and the Beginning of the Great Depression*. Capitalism Works Publishing, 2005.

Seow, Joanna, and Tham Yuen-C. "Work in Progress: Redesigning Jobs, Retooling Mindsets." *The Straits Times*, February 12, 2018, www.straitstimes.com/singapore/redesigning-jobs-retooling-mindsets.

Seow, Joanna. "Spotlight on Calculation of Income Inequality." *The Straits Times*, March 20, 2018, www.straitstimes.com/singapore/spotlight-on-calculation-of-income-inequality.

Sharma, Basu, and Irene Chew. "The Role of Compensation Policies in Singapore's Competitiveness." *Asia Pacific Journal of Human Resources* 30, no. 2 (December 1992): 16–24.

Si Guo. *Price and Wage Flexibility in Hong Kong SAR*. Washington, DC: International Monetary Fund Asia and Pacific Department, 2017.

Siebert, Horst. "Labor Market Rigidities: At the Root of Unemployment in Europe." *Journal of Economic Perspectives* 11, no. 3 (August 1, 1997): 37–54.

"Singapore," *2019 Index of Economic Freedom*, The Heritage Foundation, www.heritage.org/index/country/singapore.

Snowdon, Brian, and Howard R. Vane. *Modern Macroeconomics: Its Origins, Development and Current State*. Cheltenham, UK: Edward Elgar, 2006.

References

Teo, Josephine. "Opinion: Why There's No Minimum Wage in Singapore." *HRD Asia*, 7 November 2018, www.hcamag.com/asia/news/general/opinion-why-theres-no-minimum-wage-in-singapore/153751.

Wan, David, and Chin Huat Ong. "Compensation Systems in Singapore." *Compensation & Benefits Review* 34, no. 4 (July 2002): 23–32.

Weitzman, Martin L. "Business Forum: Wage Rigidity Is the Central Problem." *New York Times*, May 26, 1985.

Weitzman, Martin L. *The Share Economy: Conquering Stagflation*. Cambridge: Harvard University Press, 1984.

Weitzman, Martin L., and Douglas Kruse. "Profit Sharing and Productivity." In *Paying for Productivity: A Look at the Evidence*. Edited by Alan S. Blinder. Washington, DC: Brookings Institution, 1990.

White, Lawrence H. *The Clash of Economic Ideas: The Great Policy Debates and Experiments of the Last Hundred Years*. Cambridge: Cambridge University Press, 2012.

Zongxian Yu and Dianqing Xu. *From Crisis to Recovery: East Asia Rising Again?* Singapore: World Scientific, 2001.

About the Authors

MICHAEL SZPINDOR WATSON is an assistant professor of economics and the director of the Philosophy, Politics, and Economics program at Belmont Abbey College in North Carolina. His research interests include the relationship between the Catholic intellectual tradition and economics, the history of money and banking, and the history of Poland. He enjoys skiing, dancing, singing, hunting, martial arts, marksmanship, folk cultures, and traveling to Poland and elsewhere.

GRATTAN BROWN is a Roman Catholic theologian and the academic dean of Thales College in Raleigh, North Carolina. He has written and taught about Catholic moral theology and capitalism, democracy, and bioethics and has collaborated with professionals of religious and secular backgrounds in healthcare, business, and criminal justice. Read more at https://www.whereiswisdom.today/.

www.ingramcontent.com/pod-product-compliance
Lightning Source LLC
Chambersburg PA
CBHW050330120526
44592CB00014B/2120